Who Says A Fish Can't Sell?

True Tales From Top Salespeople

Jim Cornbleet

Who Says A Fish Can't Sell?
True Tales From Top Salespeople
Jim Cornbleet
Network For You, Inc.

Published by Network For You, Inc. St. Louis, MO

Editor: Bill Motchan

Cover Illustration: Kai Chatten (Jim's seven-year-old grandson)

Cover and Interior design: Davis Creative, DavisCreative.com

Publisher's Cataloging-In-Publication Data
(Prepared by The Donohue Group, Inc.)

Names: Cornbleet, Jim, author.
Title: Who says a fish can't sell? : true tales from top salespeople / Jim Cornbleet.
Description: St. Louis, MO : Network For You, Inc., [2019]
Identifiers: ISBN 9781733782500 (paperback) | ISBN 9781733782517 (ebook)
Subjects: LCSH: Sales personnel--Anecdotes. | Selling--Anecdotes. | LCGFT: Anecdotes. | BISAC: BUSINESS & ECONOMICS / Sales & Selling / General. | BUSINESS & ECONOMICS / Sales & Selling / Management. | BUSINESS & ECONOMICS / Motivational.
Classification: LCC HF5439.5 .C67 2019 (print) | LCC HF5439.5 (ebook) | DDC 658.85--dc23

To my family:
who have stood beside me
throughout the years.
I love you.

Table of Contents

Foreword

Let's get one thing straight. Most people in our world aren't capable of being a productive salesperson. When they hear *No,* it sticks in their heads, right between their eyes. They take *No* personally! A real salesperson lets *No* go in one ear and out the other, then concentrates on convincing the prospect that he/she has the best solution for their needs.

I worked with Jim Cornbleet, the author of this book, for many years. He heard a lot of *Nos* but most often he found a way to show his prospect the true value of his solution. If your career is dependent on your ability to sell, you have got to read this book! You will learn a lot, and you will laugh a lot. I promise!

Jimmy will describe the real world life of a salesperson. He will offer tips and lessons learned that will enable you to be more productive. He will reveal many behind-the scenes struggles of real salespeople. As I've already said, get ready to learn and laugh!

James A. Grimmet, Jr.

Jim Grimmet has been in sales for more than 40 years serving as an IBM account executive, Amdahl senior vice president and an Edward Jones financial advisor.

Preface

There's nothing quite like closing a sale.

It's hard to describe the emotional boost you get from your first success as a salesperson. Of course, there's a financial benefit from your commission, but most sales professionals I've met love the adrenalin rush of the close.

What can I compare it to? A runner's high. Your first kiss. Seeing the majesty of the Grand Canyon.

To be successful in sales requires a special mindset. I believe you have to approach every customer opportunity with optimism. Understand that there will be obstacles. Your customer may a have longtime relationship with a competitor who has a topnotch salesperson. But if you believe in yourself, your company and your product and you listen and build trust with the customer, you can win.

Much has been written about the sales process and how to succeed. In this book, I have highlighted sales successes from my own career and from other salespeople who I respect and admire.

Here's a little insight into my approach to sales. I believe the more information you have about your customer, the better armed you'll be. I'm talking about little details, like the decision-maker's hobbies, spouse's name, what grade their kids are in.

What does that have to do with the product you're selling and the customer's needs?

Absolutely nothing.

But by gaining the confidence of the person who will be instrumental in selecting a winning bid, that little extra information could be extremely valuable. That's because a great salesperson must know how to do three things: be a good listener, build trust and deliver on what you say.

Closing a sale is often a matter of how you present yourself and your product. If you do it with confidence, it will radiate and your customer will recognize that you believe in what you're selling. Also, it's important to remember you're not just there as a salesperson for a one-shot opportunity. Ideally, you want to develop a long-term relationship.

That's a very short and simple summary of my outlook and philosophy of sales. I am an avid reader about the sales process, and I always enjoy learning new skills and techniques. As you read the stories that follow, you'll notice that I have called out in boldface type where I or my colleagues discovered **key lessons learned.** In fact, when you get to chapter 11, you'll find a baker's dozen **key lessons learned** from fascinating salespeople I interviewed when I began this journey over 14 years ago.

I invite you to read on and I hope you'll gain some valuable insights from the stories I have to share. Thanks and happy selling!

Designed by Katemangostar / Freepik

Chapter 1

Pushing The Envelope

When you experience some success in sales, a natural progression is getting promoted to management. It's great to be recognized for your accomplishments and take on added responsibility. I began working at Amdahl in 1987, and very quickly I helped close some big sales. The first was Monsanto in 1988, followed by General Dynamics the following year. We were on a roll, creating momentum and establishing our reputation as a major competitor in the growing market for computer processors.

I was rewarded for my tenaciousness and sales prowess by a promotion from account executive to management. That didn't make me less focused on closing a sale. It did give me some important insight: You have to balance meeting the customer's needs with the long-term financial viability of your own company.

A good example of this was when we closed our first sale with May Department Stores (which was acquired by Federated Department Stores in 2005 and has since been rebranded as Macy's).

At the time, May had data centers around the country, one of which was in St. Louis where my team was located. We met on a number of occasions with the director of the data center and his staff. On our initial bid, we lost to a competitor, so we followed up by visiting May's senior VP as a postmortem, to learn what we did right and how we could improve on the next go-round.

This process made a lot of sense. Instead of fretting about the loss and cursing the fates, we took the initiative to do better by going to the source. It demonstrated a level of maturity and a willingness to learn. One of the takeaways from that meeting was that the consumer retail business operates on a slim margin and that even the buyer we were calling on would consider buying from a competitor.

The big players like May are leaders because they squeeze every penny of profit out of their operations. I knew this because Wayne showed me a daily report once that their execs had to review—it was essentially a spreadsheet with a seemingly endless list of numbers, indicating the tight budgets they operated within. To gain a spot as a vendor, you'd better be willing to offer them a great deal.

The following year, we sized up the competition and we offered May a creative solution—a second generation processor. It would be enticing from a budget perspective and it was every bit as good as what IBM was offering. Our goal was to get our product in the door and demonstrate our commitment to service after the sale.

Things were looking up when I got an important call to meet with Wayne. He said "You've got this deal if you make the following adjustments to your bid." I told him to hang on for just a minute and I walked outside his office to call my vice president, who just happened to be in town that day. I told my VP what we needed to change to close the deal and he said, "OK, let me get back to you in a few days." I knew time was of the essence and I could close the sale if I moved quickly. I replied, *"No, this is serious. We can get this deal done now!"*

I walked back into Wayne's office, and he was smiling because he heard me yelling at my VP (which, by the way, was either gutsy on my part or incredibly stupid). Fortunately, it worked out great. I got the concessions from my team and we closed the sale.

Looking back, there are a couple of interesting aspects and **key lessons learned** from that experience. One was the meeting we had with the customer after initially losing a bid. If a sales pitch is not working, you have to adapt. It's all about the customer and their needs. Even when you don't get the win, you make it a learning experience.

Another intriguing part of that process was that I had to convince two vastly different entities to agree to the terms of the sale. The May Company executives were ready to sign on the dotted line. I still had to sell my own team on the merits of landing this account.

It's important to have the fire and passion to close a sale, which I probably demonstrated a little too dramatically that day outside the May purchasing director's office. A year or two later I was having a drink with him, and he remembered that I yelled at my vice president. As I already mentioned, it either took guts or stupidity. Then again, a customer once told me it's good to push the envelope.

The key takeaway and **key lessons learned** from this experience is if at all possible, satisfy the customer needs promptly, be transparent and let them know what you're going through as a salesperson to satisfy their demands. At the same time, you must be cognizant that you are representing your company and you have to weigh the importance of the sale. You may take a hit on the cost of the initial sale. On the other hand, you can generate additional revenue from service and support, which is exactly what we did in this case.

"Your chances of success in any undertaking can always be measured by your belief in yourself."

– Robert Collier

Chapter 2

What Do You Have To Lose? A lot.

Sales can be a solitary endeavor. As the lead account executive, success or failure often comes down to your ability to understand your customer and deliver a compelling solution. I've been in that position on numerous occasions. And although it was my responsibility to close the sale, success from sales also includes the teams of service and support people who were ready, willing and able to provide the customer with the quality solution that was promised to be delivered.

I also have been blessed to count as friends some very fine salespeople. We learn from each other, celebrate each other's successes and commiserate when things don't go according to plan.

One of my best friends is also a top-notch salesperson named Patti Harty. In this chapter, I've asked her to share one of her memorable sales experiences that did not result in high-fives and a champagne toast. It was a sales loss, not a win. It was also a valuable learning experience for her and for anyone who aspires to succeed in this rewarding, and often humbling, line of work.

Patti never intended to go into sales. She started out in early childhood education. Then again, trying to hold the attention of a roomful of children might have been an excellent training ground and starting point for her later success. I'll let her explain in her own words how she became a great salesperson, what she's learned along the way, and the satisfaction she gets from her work.

~

My dad was in real estate sales his whole life. I never ever thought I would follow in his footsteps and go into sales. One summer I decided to get a job in the business world. At that time, I did not have any business experience, but it seemed like a good idea at age 26. And, at the time IBM was hiring like crazy so I took an employment test and I did pretty well on it. Lo and behold, they hired me. The funny thing was I joined the company on the technical side as a systems engineer, and I didn't know anything about computers, either. I quickly realized that I was more suited to sales than technical support and made that career switch.

I also didn't exactly look the part of a polished professional. I had big hair with a hippy vibe. My image was not that of a businesslike salesperson, but I did have one other quality that turned out to impact my sales success throughout my career. I am fiercely competitive. However, all strengths can become weaknesses, and I learned that sometimes you need to temper that need to win. Here's what I mean.

Early on in my sales career, after my experience at IBM, I was a senior account executive for an information technology firm. I was calling on a major Fortune 500 company. The customer had recently brought on a new director and one of my challenges was to cultivate a relationship with her. The ultimate goal was to expand our services and support with the company.

We had reason to be optimistic because we had a solid relationship and a history of delivering quality training. I had already been working with a number of groups in their technology organization over the past several years. Our future looked bright. We intended to focus on gaining a stronger foothold in the training area. What possibly could go wrong?

It's safe to say that even when you're dealing from a position of strength, winning is not a given. The newly hired director and I had our first meeting and it started badly. Something just didn't click. Maybe it was chemistry—or a lack of it. Perhaps I was overconfident, bordering on cocky, and just maybe I was too focused on winning to remember a sales basic: listen to the customer and understand his or her needs.

The weird thing is, developing relationships has always come easily to me. I chalked it up to the new director maybe having a bad day. Next time, I thought, I will work on this and improve the relationship. Unfortunately, that did not happen. Over the next meeting with the director, and the meeting after that, I tried to muster my abilities to develop a relationship. It just wasn't coming together. It was too late.

What doesn't start well, doesn't end well. And much to my chagrin, she ultimately awarded a $70,000 contract for training to another company.

In retrospect, I just didn't do a good job of reading the customer and establishing rapport. Most of all, *I should have focused on her needs.* Instead, I took on a role of the expert, the role that she viewed herself, not me. It felt like we were in a challenge match. As I look back, I saw my nature of being competitive coming through, just like in tennis, and I play a lot of tennis. When I get out on the court, even with my close friends, I put on my game face and I'm there to win. However, I was learning that's not the best way to approach a client!

I vowed it wouldn't happen to me again, and I started placing more emphasis on my skills to build trusted advisor status with my customers by really understanding and listening to their needs. I used that positive energy with my other accounts and we not only made up for the $70,000 shortfall, but generated additional new revenue from other major accounts.

∼

The lesson from that situation is that when there's a changing of the guard, you can never assume anything. You can never assume that your products and services—regardless of how good they are—will be a good fit for whoever comes in or who's new. That's why it's so important to build trust and figure out where that person is coming from. It's critical to be empathetic and a good listener. I still work on the skill of "really" listening today. You can never be a good enough listener.

Remember, though, my competitive streak had not gone away. Does a *No* mean a *No* forever? Maybe not. The president of my company and I decided to go to the CEO of the customer where we had just lost the business. "What did we have to lose," we thought.

Well, we learned that we not only had the training to lose, but we also lost other existing business in the account, due to the fact that we had gone over someone's head. Their culture was not favorable to a top down approach and our approach backfired.

That one still smarts. I think **the lesson** there is be careful when you say "What do you have to lose?" The answer could be "A lot more than you think."

As salespeople, we really prefer it when the customer says *Yes*. Most will agree on that. But what about the *Nos* like in the above situation? The *Nos* can even be more important and valuable because you learn from them. When you do lose, you fail forward.

Throughout a sales career of 30-plus years, there have been many times when I helped a client achieve success, and in the process developed a great relationship and closed sales as a result of this. That's why I love my work, and I couldn't imagine a more satisfying career than sales focused on helping others become more successful and fulfilled. I think the reason I do what I do is that it really changes people's lives personally and professionally. They feel better, they discover things about themselves, they improve themselves and improve their lives.

~

Patti Harty works for Stark and Associates, Inc., a St. Louis-based firm that is an authorized licensee of Sandler Training.

"To win. . . you've got to
stay in the game. . ."

– Claude M. Bristol

Photo by Mike Birdy

Chapter 3

Professional Persistence Pays Off

Salespeople are wired up differently than other folks. We love to relive our favorite stories of memorable sales (whether they resulted in a big win or a near-miss or an outright disaster). Most of us are outgoing and gregarious. And we are extremely competitive.

These characteristics accurately describe my friend Jeff Loeb. I love listening to him hold court on sales theory and what makes a great salesperson. It's simple and makes a lot of sense. In this chapter and in chapter 6, Jeff will share with us examples of what it takes to be a great salesperson in an extremely competitive field: the toy industry.

Jeff knows this industry well, having worked in it for close to 30 years. He started in the business as an intern for Kenner Products (then a division of the General Mills Toy Group), which developed iconic toys in the 1950s and 1960s like the Give-A-Show Projector and the Easy-Bake Oven. During Jeff's tenure there in the 1980s, the company had additional successes with Star Wars, Strawberry Shortcake and other hot toy lines.

Jeff's connections helped him land an internship at Kenner; his father was a summer camp cabin-mate of the company's then-CEO Joe Mendelsohn (who was posthumously inducted into Toy Association Hall of Fame in February 2019). Looking back on his career, Jeff admits that he learned more about what makes a great salesman from his tenure at Kenner than anywhere else he has worked since.

The toy business is not for the faint of heart. A hot must-have toy one year can quickly fizzle out. You never know what's going to capture the public's imagination. The Pet Rock rose to fame in 1975, selling 1.5 units and making its inventor a millionaire. Six months later, sales disappeared and so did the product.

Behind the scenes are salespeople like Jeff who help bring the next new toy to market. I mentioned that competitiveness is a key quality in a salesperson, and Jeff certainly exhibits that trait. I should know—he and I are co-"owners" of a fantasy football team, and I'm happy to report we were the top team in our league the last two seasons.

When I asked Jeff to describe a memorable sale in his career, he said there were several that came to mind, all of which were significant for different reasons. I'll let Jeff describe how they played out.

∽

When I think about my most memorable sales, the first one that comes to mind was when I was working for a start-up company, University Games. The year was 1987 and we got an order from Kmart, at the time one of the top three toy retailers in the country (probably the world). This was a big deal for us as, aside from adding a monumental sales lift to the company, it also impacted our manufacturing, logistical and financing capacity. When we received the computer-generated order, it must have been 12 inches high.

Receiving that order was a very exciting thing. Some of it was luck, but the reality is we did a lot of research before we went in to meet with the toy buyer. We canvassed Kmart store shelves in multiple markets focusing on display and retail pricing. After doing our homework, we concluded the only reason the buyer would be interested in doing business with us would be because they could make more money from buying our product than a product from an existing vendor.

We really did our homework—we very organized and strategic in our thinking and in what we ended up presenting to them. However, before all of this, there was a major hurdle to overcome. The buyer didn't know us from Adam. By enlisting support from some of my toy industry connections, we were able to give the Kmart toy buyer a comfort level that we weren't just some start-up company who popped up from nowhere. I had friends who had done business with Kmart and they did me the favor of telling the buyer, "I want you to meet with Jeff, he's a legitimate guy."

This got us the appointment, which by itself was gold and something few start-up companies accomplish so early in their existence…much less actually receiving an order, which we did! It was 30,000 pieces of a board game called Dinomite (featuring dinosaurs) that we sold to Kmart for $6 or $7.

There was also a public relations angle to the sale as Dinomite was created by a six-year-old boy who had won a national young inventor's contest. So, part of our presentation to Kmart was that media and PR attention would support their sales. The buyer concluded, thankfully, that Dinomite was a great new product that was promotable and where Kmart could realize a better margin return.

The key lessons learned from this Kmart sale were: do your homework, be organized and establish credibility with the buyer.

The second example is a sale made to Walmart around 2010. My company was an existing Walmart vendor, so we already had access with the toy buyer. That eliminated the overwhelming hurdle of getting an appointment with the world's #1 retailer—who is notoriously difficult to get set up with as a new supplier much less from a small company like ours.

A salesperson has 10, maybe 20 minutes to gain a Walmart buyer's attention and interest, so it is essential to identify the sweet spot well in advance of the meeting. We refer to this as the "five-minute elevator pitch." Again, doing our homework was paramount and, in this case, we got creative. We ended up presenting a program of 12 items targeted to a specific consumer demographic for select Walmart stores in select regions of the country where we believed it would sell best. Walmart allows suppliers access to their store demographic data for this very purpose…i.e., to help them run their business better.

We recommended a line of games, humorous in tone, and with appeal to rural markets and stores mostly in the southeastern U.S. The reality is that not all toy suppliers took that extra step at the time. This was probably one factor that allowed us to separate ourselves from competitors in the buyer's mind. We made a presentation and got the sale.

Another significant aspect of that sale was that we did the lion's share of the distribution analysis for the buyer. This entailed setting up products in the Walmart system, identifying specific stores where the product would display along with quantities of each title per store. Just as important was our daily tracking of sales and communication with the buyer on progress and where reorders might be warranted. In the end, the product sold well and we got repeat business.

∽

One of the key lessons learned from this experience is the importance of follow-up. I use a term that is extremely important. I call it "professional persistence." Every salesperson must be persistent but the adjective "professional" describes the fine line a salesperson walks between good follow up vs. irritating the buyer and risking the sale slipping through their hands.

"Behold the turtle. He makes progress only when he sticks his neck out."

– James Bryant Conant.

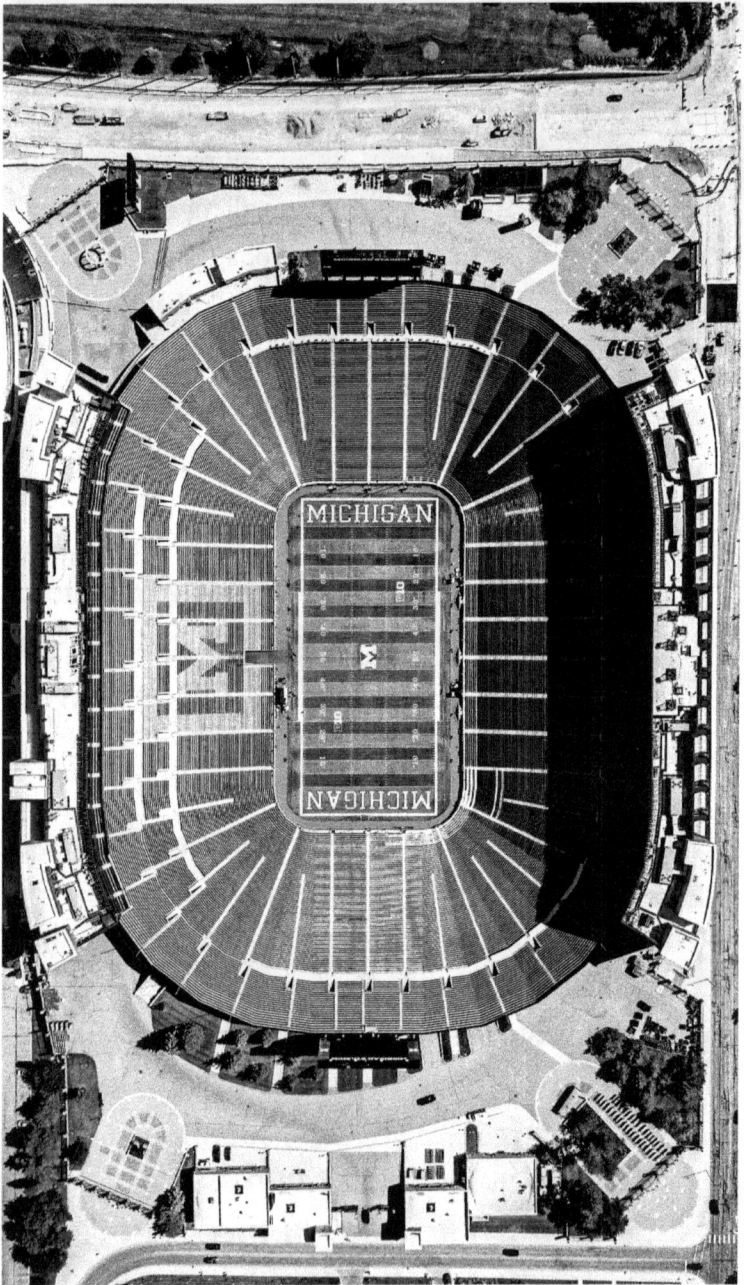

Photo by Alex Mertz

Chapter 4

At The Five Yard Line

One thing I've learned over the years about sales and salesmanship is that patience and persistence pay off just as my friend Jeff Loeb accurately stated in chapter 3. A salesperson who thrives on immediate gratification might do well to try a different line of work. Often, a successful sale is the culmination of months—or years—of prep work. Persistence gets you in the door. Patience will help carry you across the goal line.

Here's a good example of accepting and winning at a long-range strategy: I was the lead account executive at Amdahl, working with General Dynamics, the global aerospace and defense company. The customer's corporate headquarters was in St. Louis, my territory. They had three other locations in other cities, so I coordinated my efforts with our account execs serving those areas.

We were proposing a substantial technology solution for the customer, with a value of nearly $12 million. We had been working for nearly a year to educate the customer about our value-adds, which focused on service and support. My colleague Rick* in Fort Worth, Texas, worked with the head of the customer's data center there, while I met regularly with the controller, director of strategy, and vice president of information technology in St. Louis.

It's never easy for a customer to consider a technology solution that differs from their current architecture. While the customer could save money or get superior service by working with us, there's a potential for disaster. What if we can't deliver on what we're promising? The VP who signed off on the deal could lose his or her job. There's a risk in moving from the status quo, and as a salesperson, I get it. It's the classic FUD (fear, uncertainty and doubt) factor.

General Dynamics had 20 IBM processors around the country. IBM was Goliath and we were David—small yet mighty. My company provided an alternative with an important value-add: great support and service after the sale. IBM may have been the industry leader, but we kept nipping at their heels.

Our challenge was to get just one Amdahl processor installed. If we could do that, we could be well on our way to additional sales.

There was no question that IBM had the upper hand. However, they still had reason for concern. If we got even one Amdahl processor installed at General Dynamics, that might lead to a second, or third, and ultimately, we could take over the entire account. I knew that the first sale was key.

I mentioned the significance of patience and persistence. Over the course of a year, we had multiple meetings with General Dynamics executives in St. Louis. My plan was to build credibility and get their execs out to our headquarters in Sunnyvale, California. Rick and his team blanketed the data center director and his staff. He made them aware of our local service and support capabilities, and importantly, the local references who could provide valuable testimonials.

We executed the plan with finesse—and it was an important move. One of our distinguishing differences was making our senior leadership available to meet with prospective customers. I prepped our CEO beforehand and he had a comprehensive lunch meeting with the General Dynamics VP of technology. Make no mistake, IBM would also bring out a big gun. However, it probably wouldn't be their top person. They might offer up a director. By arranging a meeting with our CEO, we demonstrated how hungry we were for the business.

My prep time with our CEO was significant, too. He was a busy man, so I needed to be concise yet thorough in my briefing about the customer and our game plan for securing the business. I had autonomy in arranging these meetings, which was a huge advantage. I was like the quarterback of the team.

There's another analogy that describes the power of teamwork quite well: I used to say the members of our team were like rowers in a rowboat. We each have an oar, and we are all equally important in rowing and moving the vessel in a straight line.

Moving back to my football reference, as the quarterback of our team, I had a level of confidence in our ability, and a desire to win. We were on the five yard line and I knew the end zone was so very close. I could taste victory. It was only after numerous sessions with the customer's technical and financial crew that we secured the deal.

On June 9, 1989, I went to the controller's office and said, "You know, we're getting close." I got there at 9 a.m. and left at 3 p.m. It was a long, exhausting day. At 3 p.m., I walked out the door with a letter of intent to purchase their first Amdahl processor. I immediately called my colleague Rick to share the exciting news.

I was at General Dynamics all day to keep the momentum going. I helped them draft the letter of intent, so that I would leave with something in hand showing their commitment. Once the controller had the vice president of IT approve it, we had a deal.

As a postscript, Amdahl secured an additional $25 million in business from General Dynamics. IBM initially had 98% of the market share here in the St. Louis area for large system computers, and after 10 years, we had 40% of the share.

It all came down to relationships—relationships with the people at the data center and the relationships we created in St. Louis. It took persistence, integrity, follow up, and professionalism.

~

A key lessson learned from this experience is that salespeople should believe in themselves, their companies, and their products, in that order. People often say selling is innate; some people have it, others don't. I think it can be developed — that if you are trained and surrounded by people who are good in sales, you can pick up the necessary characteristics and skills. Then, you practice and practice. You can learn from repeated failures because you learn from everything you do. When you lose a sale, you learn to get up and try again.

I've always said that sales is the easiest, *hardest* profession in the world. If you make a mistake, they're never going to forget it. If you deliver on your commitments, and are available and responsive to the customer, you will succeed. Communication is vital. That often requires a lengthy process. The sales pitch is just words, until you earn the honor and privilege of playing in the game.

> *"Ask for money, you get advice.*
> *Ask for advice, you get money."*
>
> – anonymous

---

*Coincidently Rick's Dad, Bill was my direct manager at the time of this sale (and many others of mine described in this book). Without Bill's invaluable advice and coaching to me (and of course, to Rick while growing up) this sale and others would never have happened. Thanks again, Bill.

Chapter 5

Change The Rules And You Can Win Big

A good salesperson needs a number of skills and qualities. Just a few of those happen to begin with the letter C: cleverness, curiosity and creativity. Sometimes you'll find a customer with a very specific need that your product doesn't precisely address. That is not necessarily a sign of a dead end. Maybe you haven't considered all the possibilities.

That was exactly how my friend and former neighbor Chris Herrington came upon his most memorable sale. Chris is a gregarious guy who can start up a conversation with just about anyone. That's a great quality for a salesperson. The funny thing is, Chris started out not in sales at all. He was hired as a research chemist for Monsanto's Enviro-Chem Group. (Monsanto was acquired in 2018 by Bayer.)

Chris got the opportunity to move to a marketing job in the fast-growing Monsanto Agricultural Division. The new job was product supervisor for a product called Polaris, a plant-growth regulator for sugar cane. He did well in that position and was promoted to an area manager—not a salesperson—overseeing seven retail fertilizer plants. He was promoted again to district manager, then national sales director for industrial products. All along he was not a salesperson, yet he had salespeople and then district managers of sales who reported to him.

Those years observing the sales process and managing it were important for Chris in his development. He knew what it took to close a sale, if given the chance. He would do just that when he left Monsanto after a successful 20-year career. Chris went to the agribusiness company J.R. Simplot as a sales rep. Suddenly, he had to put his sales chops to the test. Here's a fascinating story of how he used cleverness, curiosity and creativity to change the rules and close a huge sale, growing to nearly $3 million annually. It had a good run, too, nearly a decade.

~

I was nearly 43 years old and it was my first time being a sales rep where I had to sell stuff. It was frightening for me because I had never been a salesperson. I had supervised salespeople. I never had to do it before, and now I was the guy. It was a big difference.

The product line for Simplot Industrial Products was chemical intermediates that went into the company's fertilizer line. They were mineral acids, sulfuric acid, nitric acid, those type of things. I was trying to figure out ways to market our phosphoric acid.

Through one of our distributors we found an interesting possibility—to substitute our phosphoric acid, which was a much lesser grade than food-grade phosphoric acid, in the production process for pet food. It hadn't been done before and the pricing differential was huge, but there was also the risk that it wouldn't work.

It took us two and a half years of research, going to the pet food company's headquarters, analyzing all the technical issues of whether it would work. The way pet food is produced is pretty interesting. Pet food kibbles are a soy-based product, which dogs and cats will not eat. So they trick the pets by spraying a gruel made out of chicken offal. To make the gruel, they use a digestif, usually phosphoric acid. After that, the pet food goes through a palatability test to make sure the dogs and cats will eat it.

Food-grade phosphoric acid is relatively expensive. Our product, used primarily as an intermediate for fertilizers or cattle feed, was a lower grade and cost far less. It occurred to me that it could work for pet food and to process the gruel.

Now keep in mind that chicken innards can be quite tasty. A restaurant in Potterville, Michigan, known as Joe's Gizzard City draws people from miles around. If you're into gizzards, bon appétit! The pet food company we were courting used chicken feet in the gruel for a while, but their supplier ended up getting a better price on chicken feet by selling them to China, where consumers—not dogs and cats—consider them a delicacy.

I remember going for the trials, trying the product. They took the chicken offal and innards, put them in a shredder, then added in our phosphoric acid which was the digestif; it creates a giant stomach, and it turns into this brown gruel that they spray on the kibble. After the test, we found that the process worked. Then we needed to conduct the palatability study. Everything checked out and we closed the sale.

In addition to creating a new use for the product, we had to create a logistics system from the ground up. We mined the acid in Rock Springs, Wyoming, processed it in Pocatello, Idaho, then transported it 1,500 miles by rail to St. Louis. From there, it was trans-loaded to trucks and sent to the pet food plant in southern Missouri. The plant had very limited on-site storage. If we didn't supply, the plant shut down. I became not only the technical guy, I learned a lot about logistics, and I mean a lot. It was rewarding and fun for me, because I had watched these processes from afar, and now I was the point person.

The entire process is really fascinating to look back on. The customer wasn't sure it would work. Heck, my own company wasn't convinced. I remember one guy telling me, a big muckety-muck, "Oh, we've tried that, it will never work." Of course, most good salespeople hate the phrase, "We will never" or "You will never." It actually becomes a personal challenge to prove them wrong.

Of course, if I looked at my job as just selling stuff, this sale would never have happened. It wasn't logical because the product didn't really fit on paper. We made it fit. Then the product had to go through regulatory bodies and we didn't have anybody at Simplot who knew how to do that or who could handle the testing. And of course there were challenging logistics. I was basically the guy, so learning how to do those things was fun, scary sometimes, but fun nonetheless.

I started out as a bench chemist so I was fortunate to have that background and knowledge which was very helpful. The other thing is I'm pretty good at garnering resources, and you basically are at the mercy of the lab and our product line was tiny compared to all the other things that were going on. When Simplot recognized this could be a very profitable sale, they started getting interested. And to this day—even though I've been gone for a while from there—they use that as an example of how you can find profitability from unlikely or untapped sources.

A good salesperson has to build trust and rapport. Now people say you got to have the gift of gab so the customer likes you. A customer doesn't buy from you because they like you, they buy from you because they trust and respect you. In some cases, they trust you with their jobs. The purchasing agent's life could get more complicated if you change the supply chain. There were several times it got scary but we watched every shipment and we knew where those shipments were at any given time.

❧

I think the primary lessons learned from this sale were: understanding and explaining the sales cycle and recognizing that you'll need to educate your management to be patient with that. The internal sale is almost always more difficult than the external sale. Most people don't realize that. All those negative things, you have to fight through and convince people, and you have to demonstrate positivity to the customer of course, as well as your internal people to demonstrate the potential.

The other important lesson is, if you're able to change the rules in any game, you can win and win big.

"If you don't like something change it; if you can't change it, change the way you think about it."

– Mary Engelbreicht

Photo by Chanaka

Chapter 6

Think Outside The Box

One of the fascinating aspects of sales is that you frequently find yourself serving two masters: the company you represent and your customer. Chris Herrington just offered an excellent example of that in chapter 5 when he had to convince his company that his innovative solution would work. It ended up benefitting both his company and his customer.

When you demonstrate to the customer that you want to do what's good for them, you'll create goodwill. Of course, you must make sure that first and foremost your loyalty and allegiance are with your company. That's who pays your salary and it's the brand you represent.

This duality of allegiance can make for some fascinating dynamics for a salesperson. In chapter 1, I described my own experience having to sell my company on a proposal when I knew the customer was ready to sign on the dotted line. In this chapter we are joined again by my longtime friend and comrade in arms Jeff Loeb. We first heard from Jeff in chapter 3, where he described a couple of noteworthy sales.

Jeff is a veteran of the fractious and competitive toy industry. He loves the thrill of the sale—like all of us who gravitate to this profession—and he knows the toy business better than most people.

A few years ago, he even decided to strike out on his own and create a line of toys which he's selling through both traditional retailers and via e-commerce. It's a lot of work but he enjoys every minute of it. He told me as much when I asked what he gets out of it: "I'm in control and it's my concept. I'm using all of my background and knowledge and experience to do what I know how to do best."

The toy industry is incredibly complex, and it takes someone with Jeff's knowledge to wrap your head around manufacturing, quality control, importation logistics, warehousing, order processing, sales spreadsheets and distribution channels. Fortunately, Jeff figured out a creative way to satisfy a top retailer, as you'll see in the following story.

∽

This sale was one I remember fondly. The client was T.J. Maxx, the popular retailer. T.J. Maxx is a division of TJX Companies which also owns and operates off-price retail chains including Marshalls, HomeGoods and others. TJX Companies have a value strategy whereby their stores sell brand name products at deep discount pricing which they most often accomplish by either, a) purchasing discounted goods from suppliers with excess inventory, or b) creating custom or "make-up" items (displaying the brand name) just for T.J. Maxx.

While brands like Tommy Hilfiger or Ralph Lauren usually don't like being associated with off-price retailers, from time to time their excess inventory or sub-branded products might show up at T.J. Maxx stores.

In my situation, the T.J. Maxx buyer had seen our products from the prior season in stores they competed with and they called me. It's a rarity for a buyer to call you instead of vice versa so "credibility" with them was pre-established. They liked the merchandise and I was invited to meet with their buying team (merchandise manager, buyer and assistant buyer).

I was well prepared for the meeting, having surveyed their stores in advance. I understood both their key retail price points and gross margin requirements. Also, at the time we did not have excess inventory so I knew going into the meeting that any sale would be the "make-up" of additional items (similar to what we already had in the marketplace).

The challenges of this particular sale fell into two areas:

1. Delivering product to meet T.J. Maxx retail price and gross margin targets
2. Satisfy my company's profitability requirements

So, I had two stakeholders to sell.... the customer and my company.

I was able to satisfy T.J. Maxx via a highly discounted selling price transacted on a "duty paid landed" basis whereby they took ownership of the goods once they cleared customs at the U.S. port of entry (instead of supplying through our domestic

Memphis warehouse). This helped avoid additional costs associated with inland transportation (from the west coast to Memphis), warehousing and other overhead costs normally associated with a domestic sale.

I was able to satisfy my company through a sizeable purchase amount. While our gross margin percentage on this sale was less than normal, the overall dollar profitability of the sale was acceptable and worth the effort.

Managing the entire process was far from easy. It required a lot of time and attention to detail along with continual bartering between both the customer and my company. For example, we insisted that T.J. Maxx place a large enough order in total and that every ocean shipping container sail completely full (we were paying the ocean freight from China to the U.S., so we didn't want to ship and pay for "air" or excess space in containers). To accomplish this, I made regular calls to the buyer. A typical conversation might begin, "I need you to buy an additional 250 units of product A to fill the container."

With my company, it was more cumbersome and mostly a matter of grinding out countless spreadsheets and analysis demonstrating how every penny was spent and what fell to the bottom line. The detail work associated with coordinating the shipment and quantifying the profitability was more laborious and detailed than any sales project I had ever undertaken, but it was worth it.

And I became adept at a new skill—data analyst.

The net result was one of those rare "win-win-win" situations where customer-company-end user all win. Most importantly the product sold exceptionally well and we repeated this program for years afterwards.

～

There are a few important lessons I learned from this sales experience. It's always important to do your research, be prepared, be organized and employ professional persistence in customer interactions. However, the more important lesson here is the attention to detail and endless follow up that resulted in both customer and company giving the greenlight.

"Confidence comes from competence."

— anonymous

Photo by Josh Sorenson

Chapter 7

Stay True To Your Values

When I look back at my career and memorable sales experiences, one that stands out was my first as an account executive at Amdahl. It had been a year since I left IBM. I had a drawerful of business cards and lots of notes about the customers I had called on. I wanted—and needed—one more thing: a sale.

Fortunately, my superiors were confident in my ability and they knew it took time to cultivate relationships. They treated us all like family and wanted us to succeed. It was certainly not the picture an IBM branch manager painted when I announced I was leaving Big Blue. He told me I was making the biggest mistake of my life.

I was driven to succeed. I wanted to prove that I had the skills and desire to be a great salesman, and I believed in my new company. Still, it had been a year and I had yet to close a contract. Sometimes, though, the stars align and diligence pays off. Maybe a little luck, too. This is a story of Hush Puppies, a bottle of wine and sticking with my instincts.

One of my prospective customers was Monsanto, a Fortune 500 company which we described in chapter 5. It was acquired by Bayer in 2018, and remains a major presence in the St. Louis business community. My team had spent a lot of time with Bob, the data center manager and his staff at Monsanto, educating them about our products, services and support capabilities.

Personally, it was important to me to learn everything I could about my customers. I am a disciple of sales master Harvey Mackay, who developed the "Mackay 66 Customer Profile." It's a laundry list with every possible fact about your customer, both personal and professional. In this case, I knew Bob's wife name was Jan and that he had four kids. I even knew his youngest son's nickname was "Noogie." I had lots of other pertinent business information about him, too.

A curious fact about Bob was that he seemed to have gained a level of comfort working with our systems engineer, a brilliant guy who always wore the same crepe-soled shoes known as Hush Puppies.

Bob once told me "Anybody who wears Hush Puppy shoes is a confident man and one you have to trust." Naturally, our systems engineer was by my side (with his shoes) at important meetings with Monsanto.

[As a side note, on Dec. 3, 1965, during a concert in Sacramento, California, Keith Richards of the Rolling Stones was nearly electrocuted when his guitar touched an ungrounded microphone. What saved his life? He was wearing a brand new pair of Hush Puppy boots with rubber soles that grounded him. Perhaps these shoes have some mystical properties.]

Fast forward to 1988 and about 100 miles south of Sacramento where the Stones played their electrifying show. We had just completed a full day of presentations for Monsanto at Amdahl's headquarters in Sunnyvale. We provided a detailed description of our proposed solution, featuring one of our newest mainframes. We also talked about future add-ons and answered many questions.

Following the meeting, we took our customers to dinner at a five-star restaurant in San Mateo. We were seated in the wine cellar at a long table and enjoyed some excellent vintages. We learned in a later visit at Sunnyvale with Monsanto's VP of IT that both he and our CEO were wine connoisseurs. That certainly portended well for the relationship between our companies.

One of our follow-up tasks after the big summit in California was to have a bottle of very good wine delivered directly to the Monsanto VP of IT. Our CEO didn't want to risk damaging the precious cargo. Hand-carrying it seemed to be a good plan. Kevin Hollenbach, one of my colleagues, happened to be in California the following week, and he discovered he would have a special task on his flight back to St. Louis. He nervously carried the wine with him. He was so worried that something would happen to the bottle, he was shaking. Fortunately, it got to the destination safely.

Nowadays, getting a full bottle of wine past TSA airport security might be a little tougher.

Things were looking good with our proposal and the relationship between our leaders. Then I received a call from the customer. I learned that IBM, our primary competition, was panicking. They switched gears and downgraded their offer to a used IBM processor. The director of operations at Monsanto told me what was going on and asked, "Do you want to change what you are presenting?" I replied, "No, this is what we think is best for you." We too had a used processor that we could have proposed. It just wasn't right for their applications, and it wasn't in alignment with what we'd discussed previously with the customer.

That was a key decision and it paid off. They called me up and said, "You won the deal because you did what was right for Monsanto and you didn't waver." Not only did we win the deal, our customer service after the sale was flawless; and that processor was upgraded twice and we had a relationship with them for all 15 years of my career at Amdahl.

∼

A couple of lessons learned stand out from that experience. Preparation is key, and it pays to focus on the customer's needs. I also had to have patience and cultivate a relationship with the customer. Most importantly, when the competition switched gears and changed what they were proposing, we didn't try to undercut them with a lower-priced offering. We stuck to what was best for the customer and stayed true to our values.

One of my mentors, Jim Grimmet, who wrote the foreword for this book, told me once, "You know Jim, sometimes you have to get to *No* before you get to *Yes* – and that means you have to say *No*." It's not easy to say *No* to a customer – but like Jim said, sometimes it is necessary to get to the *Yes*. I had to say *No* to something I thought was wrong for Monsanto but it sure wasn't easy at the time!

P.S.: Bob, the data center manager, and I have remained friends to this day.

> *"Don't judge each day by the harvest you reap but by the seeds you plant."*
>
> – Robert Louis Stevenson

Chapter 8

The Five Ps:
Prior Planning Prevents
Piss-Poor Performance

I have previously mentioned that I am a disciple of sales guru Harvey Mackay. That means I routinely compiled information about my customers using the "Mackay 66 Customer Profile." The list includes everything from the customer's favorite hobby to a favorite vacation destination, favorite restaurant and even favorite menu item. I recently showed my daughter Molly the Mackay 66. She rolled her eyes and said, "That explains a lot about why you are the way you are."

Of course I took that as a compliment—I love to learn about people and what makes them tick. Those are qualities that great salespeople usually exhibit. You have to figure out what your customer's goals and aspirations are in order to understand how they think.

That's also the approach used by Pam Fisher, a successful and accomplished sales director who retired from AT&T 11 years ago. Pam started out her career placing orders for pink Princess phones. She worked her way up to a supervisory role, moved to project management and eventually found her calling (if you'll pardon the pun) in sales.

Pam was a natural salesperson because she enjoys talking to people and listening to them. She had many memorable sales experiences throughout her 35-year career. One of those stands out. It's noteworthy because Pam took the time and effort to really understand her customer's needs. She wanted to make the person she was selling to shine with the latter's superiors, too. Remember what I said about understanding your customer and their goals? Toward the end of the bidding process, things got interesting. The actual delivery of the bid—a seemingly simple activity—took an unusual turn. I'll let Pam describe how it played out.

❧

My most memorable sale was to a customer that I had established a very good relationship with. The segment of customers I concentrated on were in the healthcare industry. In this case, I was dealing primarily with a woman who was the technology manager at a hospital. She and I had developed a good relationship, and they were building up their infrastructure.

The bid I was working on was in response to an RFP, which was really difficult because very often a customer had to select the low bidder. As a large Bell operating company, we weren't necessarily going to be able to bid lower than the competition. On this bid, we had an opportunity to be creative, so it wouldn't necessarily be evaluated by the bottom line price.

I had to work with a group that developed the pricing and they didn't deliver it to me until very late in the process. When I received it, I didn't like it at all. I sent it back to the pricing team and said, "Tweak this, tweak that," and they got it back to me an hour before I had to deliver the bid. With RFP responses, when they say it has a 3 p.m. deadline, they mean it. If you bring it at 3:05, you're out.

So I got the pricing, I put it in the binder, and I jumped in my car. Naturally, it's raining buckets, and I drive 45 minutes to the other side of town, and I go flying in with the binder. The floor was slick and I dropped it. Paper went flying everywhere, so I picked everything up and I literally had five minutes before the deadline to reassemble it. The technology manager I had established a relationship with couldn't do anything for me because it would have given us an unfair advantage, since she would be selecting the winning bid.

Her assistant came out and thankfully helped me put everything back in its place and I got it in on time, with seconds to spare. I won the bid and in the aftermath of that crazy day I really had to stop and think about the whole experience. I knew I wasn't the low bidder. I also knew that with a little bit of creativity in the bid, we were able to get the contract.

The moral of the story is that she trusted me. I knew her kid's names and other information about her. There was more to it. What she really knew was that I would be there whether it was to put wet pages in a binder or through the project management phase. I knew who she was and what she wanted to do.

~

There's another lesson learned from that sale. I understood the organization and what they wanted but just as important, my customer was a woman in a traditional man's job and she had a lot to prove in her organization, so my goal in dealing with her was to make her look good. We put together a proposal that she could be proud of and her boss would pat her on the back and say "Good job!" Beyond understanding the corporate goals and what they wanted to accomplish, I had to understand how to sell to them.

We always say "Understand your customer." What we're really talking about is emotional intelligence, putting yourself in the shoes of the customer and have the emotional intelligence to understand where they want to go.

It's also critical to be prepared. I had a mantra I called "The five Ps," which stood for "Prior Planning Prevents Piss-Poor Performance." I would not let my sales team out the door to give a presentation without, at the very least, putting an outline together. More often, we would go through the entire presentation. The customer knows when a salesperson is just rattling on. You have to know your material *and* present it in a cohesive, understandable way.

*"Discipline yourself, and
others won't need to."*

– John Wooden

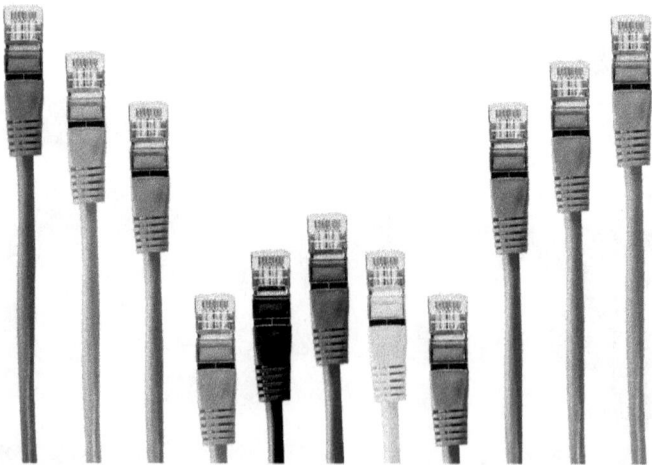

Photo by Pixabay

Chapter 9

I Thought All Salespeople Were Slimeballs

Salespeople tend to be a bit more competitive than folks in other professions. There's a thrill-of-the-chase feeling when you know you're getting close to a win. If you love to win and hate to lose, whether playing softball, golf, or a "friendly" game of Scrabble, you might have the makings of a great salesperson.

You could certainly describe this chapter's guest sales expert as competitive. He is also incredibly smart, gregarious and wickedly funny. Again, pretty good qualities for a sales professional. That's Kevin Hollenbach.

I first met Kevin when we were sales colleagues at Amdahl. We made a great team. When we called on a customer, I knew all about the buyer's personal interests, details of his or her family, favorite drink and what made them tick as a person. Kevin honed in on the customer's business need, and he could articulate our product's strengths with authenticity and credibility.

It helped that he was an engineer long before he was a sales guy. So he talked the talk and knew what he was talking about. We closed some important sales because our strengths complemented each other. More than a decade later, we remain friends, and we still reminisce about our war stories.

Since we worked together, Kevin has risen up the ranks to become regional vice president of the Central U.S. region for a leading technology solutions provider. Kevin has a unique perspective on the art and craft of sales. He shares those thoughts along with an inside look at the peculiarities of selling in a rapidly changing technology market.

∼

As a young Director of IT at BlueCross Blue Shield of Missouri, I was responsible for all purchases for the network. This was during the explosion of networking and a slew of modem salespeople jockeyed to get meetings with me. Most of them did not even know their product much less anything about our needs. I concluded that all salespeople are slimeballs.

That all changed when I got recruited to work at Amdahl as a pre-sales technical engineer. It was at Amdahl that I met outstanding salespeople like Jim Cornbleet who were all trained at IBM. Jim was the consummate relationship guy but a little light on the technology (just joking!).

Others in the office had engineering backgrounds but developed great personalities to complement the technical skill. One rep we called "the chameleon" because of the way she could relate to any customer with the right persona. After working with all of these crazy personalities that were all awesome at their craft, I realized that sales is an honorable profession and if you do it right you can make a great living and help customers succeed.

When I think back on my most memorable sales, three of them stand out.

A Bleak Christmas

The first involves none other than Jim Cornbleet. We were calling on Boatmen's Bank, which at one time was one of the 30 largest bank holding companies. It was acquired by NationsBank in the late 90s and subsequently became part of Bank of America.

The way I remember it, the buyer's name was Tony. It was getting close to the end of the year and Jim badly needed a sale. Fortunately, he had a pretty good relationship with Tony. Jim and I were in Tony's office and Jim gets out these figurines of his daughters. He said, "Tony, I really need this transaction. My kids need Christmas, so if you could do me a favor and get this transaction done, I'd really appreciate it."

Tony played along. He reached over to grab his trash can and took Jim's figurines and tossed them in and said, "Well Cornbleet, that's terrific but if I don't do the right thing for the bank, not only will my kids not get Christmas this year, but they won't ever again because I'll get fired."

Jim did get the transaction and made his all-important end of the year sale. The funniest part of it was that when we were finished talking to the buyer, Jim said "Um, can I get my figurines back?"

The lesson there was that Jim and the buyer had the kind of relationship that allowed them to have a little fun. Those types of relationships don't happen overnight. There's another aspect of that incident that's significant. In today's world, people dance around the idea that they're salespeople. The customer knows why you're there. You're not going to close a sale if you don't ask the customer for the business.

The Competition Blinked

Here's an example from when I worked for Juniper. We wanted a piece of the lucrative ethernet switching market, which is a $20 billion market. Cisco had owned that market for a long time with a 75% share which is unheard of for a technology segment. Up until about 2004, Juniper was only in the router space, which is known as "layer 3" versus switching which is "layer 2." Cisco's switching architecture at the time encompassed three "layers" of products: the access layer, aggregation layer and core layer.

Many vendors tried and failed to gain much share in the ethernet switching market. Time and again these companies would get to 1% to 2% of share and Cisco would basically put an edict out that it would not lose. If it came down to it they would match the price that most of these companies would use to try to get in. It was clear as Juniper entered this market we would have to do something other than just trying to be lower cost.

At Juniper we had this concept known as "survival of the fittest idea" (also called "healthy debate") where we would engage all levels to solve a tough problem. We engaged one of these meetings in my central region to address this challenge of how to attack Cisco in their largest market.

My engineers were emphasizing that our differentiator was in our software because it was the same at any layer of the network (access, aggregation or core) versus Cisco where each layer was actually a different business unit and the software had different features. We kept asking the question—what does this mean for customers? What is the business benefit of our software? Finally, one of the typically very quiet engineers came up with the "aha" moment—"We don't need that aggregation layer!"

This was the breakthrough we were looking for. Instead of competing on price, we competed on architecture. We took a new model to customers that REDUCED the number of ethernet ports needed to run the network by at least one-third!

When we took this concept to market one of two things happened. The "Cisco shops" refused to engage on a new design which was actually a great qualification exercise. With a $20 billion market it was easy to just walk away from customers like that who refused to think differently. Many customers loved the concept and we started winning big. We always knew we had a winning transaction when Cisco would change their bid to match our architecture. At that point we could simply ask the customer if they really believe Cisco was doing what was in their best interest all this time. Why not bid that long before we showed up?

The big lesson there was you've got to find your differentiator outside of price because you'll never compete on price alone. The **other key lesson** from that experience is one I learned early at Juniper and that was the concept of *survival of the fittest idea and healthy debate*. We had a culture that I loved where titles were left at the door and where you got into a room to brainstorm and come up with great ideas. It's a culture that's rare to find and cultivate but if you have it, you can be incredibly successful.

The New Year's Eve Miracle

My first memorable sale when I joined my current company was with a customer in Kansas City. We had just released a software-only version of our core product and had very little experience in the field actually selling it. The industry was moving to a software-only approach and it has accelerated now with the advent of public cloud. The customer came to me and said they wanted to do likewise, but they found our cost would be far higher. They said, "If we buy this solution with your hardware, it will be $3.5 million, and if we buy it with your software, it will be $30 million. Oh, and we really want to move to software."

I was new in the job. I'd only been there a few months, and I really needed a sale. Actually, my company badly needed it, too, to make its margin because we were nearing the end of the quarter.

So my response to the customer was to say, "What if I could deliver that software solution for $3.5 million? Would you buy it?" And they said they would seriously consider it.

Now I had no earthly clue if we could get the price there but I wanted to test how serious they were. I also knew strategically that we wanted to get the deal done and I knew that margins were very high on software and that inherently we had a pricing problem.

I worked with the number two man to the CFO for the customer and we were getting down to the wire. New Year's Eve, the last day we could book an order for our quarter, was on a Monday and the customer called me the Friday before with "one more thing." He wanted our maintenance discounts committed in writing for three years.

Once again, remembering my mentorship from Jim Grimmet, I would not "give" anything without a "get" so I asked the customer if we could get this last concession approved, can we get the transaction done by 10 a.m. New Year's Eve morning? That was because we would need time to process the order to ensure a clean booking for the quarter.

He said "Kevin, do you see those 35 people outside my office—do you know what they do? They cut orders at my direction so yeah, I can get you an order cut on New Year's

Eve." I found out where he would be that day (at a soccer field), got his contact information, and then we convened a war room to flesh out the details. I called the buyer on New Year's Eve, told him we delivered what he wanted, and got the deal done. It also saved the damn quarter for my company and I built myself a lot of credibility.

~

I think the big lesson learned there was that as you charge into new markets you need to listen to the customer and make adjustments that are supported by facts in the field. I've been very fortunate to work for a few companies in my career that are very good at this. Ones that listen and respond to real customer requirements are rewarded with consistent growth and staying power. The other lesson is more the basics of negotiation which frankly is sometimes a lost art. It needs to be a two-way street—no concessions without commitments—a lesson I learned from Jim Grimmet and Jim Cornbleet—sometimes you have to get to *No* before you get to *Yes*.

"Discipline is the bridge between goals and accomplishments."

– Jim Rohn

Chapter 10

The Fish

Every sales success is memorable. The same holds true for a loss, a could-have-been, should-have-been. You learn something from the experience and ideally that learning will be useful the next time around.

And speaking of learning, one of the most important tools you'll ever have in your arsenal is information—knowledge about your customer. I mean personal information about the decision maker. The other intangible you need to reach for is trust. To demonstrate how valuable it can be to learn what makes that person tick, let me share a story of how my team finally cracked a tough bid after coming up short twice.

The customer was one of the biggest railroads in the country. They were accepting bids for a big mainframe computer. My firm was bidding on equipment and a contract worth $7.2 million. We were hungry for the business and as lead salesperson, I knew what a big score like this would do for us, and for me.

I also knew all too well that it wouldn't be an easy sale. It was time for the customer's annual competition, which also marked our third time bidding. We had lost to different competitors the previous two years.

When the customer announced its third annual competition, I met with the vice president who oversaw the bidding process. He looked me in the eye and said, "I guess you won't be bidding this time." I, in turn looked him in the eyes and replied, "I'm not going anywhere. As long as you let us compete, we'll be here."

I meant it, too. I was confident that we would win eventually. It certainly wouldn't be easy. We already had lost bids to strong competitors. And, the customer's point person—the VP of technology—was a master negotiator. There were also a number of unknowns. Our competitors didn't know whether we were proposing new or used equipment, and whether to sell their top of the line or lesser line, but we could be a notch above them in other ways. We weren't usually the lowest bidder, but we could offer an after-the-sale service package to sweeten the deal.

The negotiation process for this type of bid is a high-stakes chess game. We always developed a competitive offering, and I know our bid was excellent the first two years, but the other bidders had great products and good people working for them, too.

Year three turned out to be our lucky charm. Here's how it played out.

The turning point was getting the primary director of the data centers on our side. We had been working with him and his people and we had many meetings over the first two years. Those didn't culminate in success but the process was important in establishing rapport and trust.

In the third year, we had a crucial meeting. It was just three of us in a room: me, Kevin Hollenbach (who we met in chapter 9), our systems engineer and Rich, the customer's director of data systems. He was asking us some pretty tough questions and the tension in the room was palpable. Rich was a very serious guy who worked long hours. He did have one passion away from work, though he loved to go fishing. I knew this because I made it my business to learn everything I could about a customer.

At one point in our discussion, I said something that Rich obviously didn't agree with. I could see it on his face. So I picked up my briefcase and pulled out a fish puppet. I put it on my hand and I said, "That wasn't me talking—the fish made me say it."

It was a spur-of-the-moment decision on my part to loosen the tension. My intuition paid off. The gesture made everyone smile and more importantly, we had an open, productive discussion. This was after Kevin had to pick himself up off the floor as he didn't see that coming!

Incidentally, I don't usually carry props in my briefcase. A few nights earlier, I happened to be at a get-together at a coworker's home. I saw the fish puppet there and I said, "Oh, I have to take this with me." I'm not sure why I did. Maybe it was intuition. Nevertheless, that day in our meeting, Rich couldn't help but drop his game face and laugh.

Three weeks later, I was called down to the VP's office. The previous two years in our follow-up meetings, he usually said something like, "It was a tough decision and you did great, but we plan to go with a different vendor." This time it was different. Bob smiled and tossed me an 8-inch by 12-inch envelope. He asked me to open it. Inside was a railroad T-shirt. Then he said, "Join our team."

He told me we'd won the bid for $7.2 million, and he asked our team to come down the next week and get things rolling.

As a post-script, we enjoyed a good run with the customer from that point on. We delivered on everything we promised, and they rewarded our efforts with three more contracts worth more than $15 million. **A key takeaway and key lesson learned** from this experience is that relationships are crucial, and it may take a while to find the right button to win the customer over. That fish puppet wasn't solely responsible for making a multi-million dollar sale, but it was symbolic of our tenacity and willingness to work with the customer. Most importantly, it was about understanding the customer and gaining his trust.

"Passion makes money."

— Anonymous

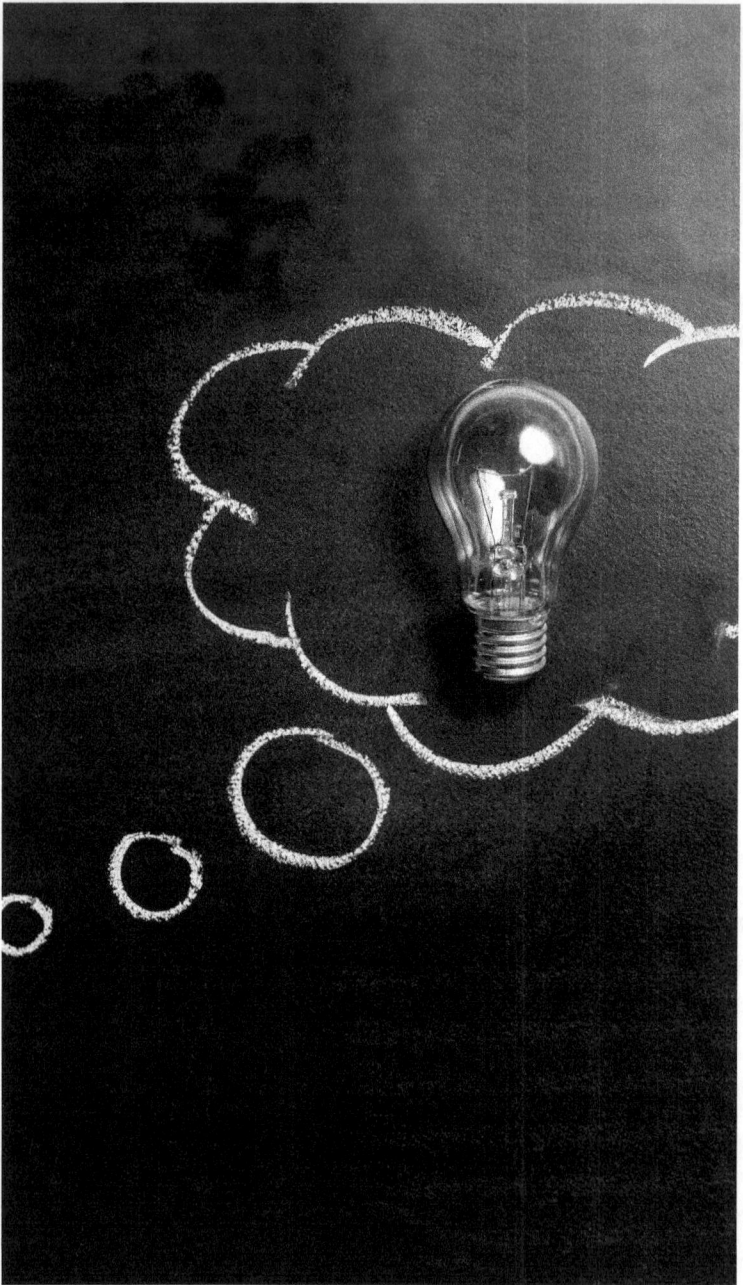

Chapter 11

What They Learned

My hope is that this book helps other salespeople understand the roller coaster ride that is this wonderful, fulfilling profession.

One of my first research steps when I conceived this project was to pick the brains of successful salespeople. Some of them I knew personally and respected.

Their experiences were so fascinating, I gave them an opportunity to relive those harrowing, exciting sales which were detailed in previous chapters.

I also spoke with a number of veteran salespeople some of whom I was not previously acquainted. These masters of the art of sales were generous with their time and provided great insight into the thought process a salesperson goes through. They shared their candid and unvarnished experiences, including – most importantly – **what they learned.** Their insights follow.

∼

Suzie Andrews – Account Manager
Suzie worked on large corporate accounts for a payment services company, a notoriously cutthroat business. Selling check

guarantee services was extremely competitive. Suzie's goal was to close a national account. After reviewing her territory, she decided to target one of the biggest accounts in the country. Her challenge was formidable. No other individual in the company had any contacts or previous experience with the prospect. On the other hand, it was a tremendous opportunity.

I did my homework, mapped out the organization, and identified the decision maker. Knowing there were many competitors, I felt it was going to take something special to even get in the door. I tried everything to get an appointment with him: first phone calls…no response. Then follow-up letters…again, nothing. More phone calls…no luck. I was determined to get in to see this man, feeling confident that once I was there, I could convince him we had a great offering.

Finally, with nothing to lose, I went to a wonderful bakery and asked them to bake a huge cookie in the shape of a clock, with the following inscription: "IT'S TIME FOR US TO MEET." I stapled multiple business cards all around the perimeter of the box and delivered the package to Mr. Decision Maker early on a Tuesday morning. Later that day, I received a phone call from him. To my surprise, he asked if I could meet him the following day.

Well, he must have loved cookies, or admired my creativity. I was never sure which. We had our meeting the following day, and it was the start of a wonderful business relationship. Soon after we met, I signed the largest deal of the year, and of my career.

What I learned: Think outside the box, or in this case, put the right message in the box. Find out what appeals to the customer, and do something no one else has done.

~

Hal Becker – Noted sales and customer service speaker and author of two best-sellers

Hal has risen to the top in three distinctly different industries. People often ask him about his secret for success in rising to the top in those fields. His answer is simple – focus and persistence.

In my first job at Xerox, I received incredible sales training. My game plan was basic: Make twenty new business calls every day, 100 a week, 400 a month. I kept calling and developing new prospects all the time. Since I always kept a minimum of 30 prospects, that ensured I would never have a bad month or quarter. It was like a diet or workout program. The only way this approach succeeded was by doing it all the time, with no breaks, no exceptions.

In fact, the best sales of my life were during a blizzard in 1978 when all local businesses were closed. Rather than lose that time, I went out in the snow knocking on doors. The only people at work were the bosses. They invited me in and gave me some coffee. We talked, and they bought 23 copy machines from me in the next three days, which is still a record at Xerox.

Focus and persistence were also key to my next venture, which was Direct Opinions. The company featured a fantastic new idea: customer follow-up telemarketing. There was just one problem. Because it was a new idea, I needed people to try something that had no track record.

Again, I made nonstop business calls, including a free trial offer of 20 telemarketing calls. I wouldn't give up until they at least tried the service. After all, how could anyone say no to something without trying it first? Today, the company conducts millions of calls each year from offices across the country.

This winning formula worked again when I wanted to become an author and lecturer. My book wasn't accepted by the first publisher who read it or by the next 15. And once it was printed, people didn't automatically flock to buy it. So I sent a free book to 3,500 major businesses, figuring the CEO would read it or give it to the VP of sales. Since then, I've personally sold tens of thousands of books and averaged more than 165 speaking engagements yearly.

What I learned: Remember, whatever your business or industry, simply concentrate on focus and persistence and you'll have your own secret for success.

~

Bev Berner – Advertising Account Executive

When Bev carefully studied her company's strategic plan, she discovered the key to closing a sale. She put together a proposal and sold her boss on it first, then took the concept to her client.

I developed the idea, worked with the creative group to bring it to life, and worked with the media department to put a plan together. Then I sold the whole concept to the client—and brought in an extra $1 million in billing on an existing $6 million account.

What I learned: It's important to have a sincere curiosity about the business and a desire to help people—clients included. You also need great listening skills and persistence.

~

Adam Capes – Co-founder & president of G2G Collection

After they graduated from Cornell, Adam Capes and Josh Goodhart moved to Atlanta and launched a lifestyle magazine called Jezebel. *Their major mission was to get advertising to support the publication and distribution of the magazine. One of their primary targets was a local car dealership. Adam and Josh knew that advertising in their magazine would offer the car dealership an awareness tool to get customers in the door. They hadn't had much luck because a secretary/gatekeeper in the auto dealership was blocking their access to the decision maker.*

After much discussion with the secretary, I realized that the decision-maker didn't have time to meet with us, and that was his loss. We threw the ball back to the secretary and decided to move on. Lo and behold, when we got back to the office, there was a phone call from the general manager saying he would like to meet with us to discuss advertising.

At that moment, we felt very optimistic. We had the appointment, and we knew that once we presented our case, the benefits would become obvious. We had taken a risk by walking out the door, but it had paid off. Maybe he thought we were not just run-of-the-mill salesmen or that we really believed in our product. Whatever it was, he agreed to see us, and the rest was up to us. By the end of that meeting we had closed the sale.

What I learned: There is always a way to make a sale… if you find a need. Later, when I thought about it, I remembered hearing my marketing professor's mantra: "Find a need and fill it!" That became our mantra. **The other lesson** was that it pays to do something different. We broke the pattern when we left. We challenged expectations, and maybe we were even a little cocky. Who says, "It's his loss" and gets the sale? We did.

~

Tom Cohn – Insurance sales, Thomas Cohn Associates

Tom has been a successful life insurance salesman since 1975 so he's experienced a lot. His current challenge was to help a widow (let's call her Sandy) solve her financial needs. Sandy's husband was a very dominant personality and had failed to successfully plan, mainly because he really did not want to take advice from anyone. Tom was introduced to the case through a family friend, which is very unusual for him as most of his business comes through attorneys.

Sandy's total assets exceeded $60 million and she had a very significant estate tax problem. My challenge was to come up with a solution to help all the family members. After reviewing the overall parameters of the situation, my initial thoughts were to propose a solution resulting in $1.2 million premium with a death benefit of $35 million. She had two daughters so after further deliberations, I decided to have each daughter pay a $1 million premium which they could finance through loans and some other outside means.

I structured the transaction over five years, not knowing what the appropriate time period I should propose. In the insurance business one often finds people selling these programs which are ostensibly going to last forever. Truly, this was in the back of my mind but the reality of it is that I have rarely seen people stick with the same program. I wanted to show them how they can get out of the policy at the end and what they needed to do to keep it going. I felt confident this was the right approach for Sandy and her family.

I went to the family to present the plan. They appeared to understand the overall concept. I could see they were excited about the benefits and were pleased with the simplicity and short time frame. I left the meeting satisfied and now needed to get the legal and financial blessing. Fortunately, the attorney and I had a previous relationship, which made his review very easy (for a lawyer), and he agreed with the plan.

The accountant was the final piece of the puzzle. He had some questions at the outset and soon realized the merits of the proposal. All parties were now in favor of moving forward. Most importantly, the family was thrilled as I had resolved how the tax liability would be paid, at least in the next five years. I had to incorporate everything I had learned over the years which was very satisfying: understanding the client's needs, using creativity, bringing in the proper resources and devising a solution that was win-win (plus, it paid a nice commission!).

What I learned: Success in sales is closely tied to success in life. Salespeople should be money motivated. How much is a lot of money? It all depends. The person will have extraordinarily high expectations built in by life experiences. Some things fall in your lap and it is up to you on how successful you want to be. Fear and lack of alternatives drive a successful person. How does your client see you? If it's positive, that determines success. Make it a win-win for you and your client. Some successful people make it win-win-win (the client, the individual and the company; here is always a balance). Be creative in developing solutions. Building relationships are key. Understand your strengths. Be in control and determine priorities. Is product knowledge important? Not necessarily. Give the client what they ask for and provide the best that is on the market. There is no best answer, there are a lot of good answers.

Patrick Garrett – Vice President of Digital Strategy at SteadyRain

Patrick is great at explaining what he does and asking the consumer the questions that will help him determine the best product. He comes across more like a friend than a salesperson, and that is important. His role at an e-learning company was as the consultative sales representative. UBS Warburg, one of the world's largest investment banking companies, presented the e-learning company a tremendous opportunity. But it was probably too late. Patrick and his team got the request for quote (RFQ) to develop an e-learning project with an unusually large amount of video content. RFQs do not typically provide a lot of details, and that was exactly what he faced.

We responded to their proposal even though we had received it very, very late in the game. In fact, we only had three days to turn it around. Diligently doing all we could in a short amount of time, we prepared our response to their proposal as best we could but felt we had to do something special. In a bold move, we decided to write a lengthy cover letter, explaining the reasons why even though UBS Warburg had stated that they were going to select a vendor strictly from the RFQ responses, we lobbied heavily for a meeting before they made their selection.

We felt this was a gutsy call. The project's target audience was investment bankers who annually received seven-figure bonuses and were accustomed to vendors doing things the bankers' way.

To our amazement, we received a call the day after we delivered the proposal. They asked if we could be at their headquarters the next day. Something must have intrigued them or at least they were curious and impressed enough that we would ask for a meeting to explain our proposal. So of course, we arranged flights and arrived in Connecticut for our meeting.

Walking into the facility, I thought this is pretty cool, four Midwesterners amongst the titans of the investment world. I had to admit we were a bit intimidated by the surroundings. In fact, I was awestruck by the grandeur of the place. We were led into a conference room with 20 foot high ceilings. Someone pressed a button, and the whole far end wall opened up. All of sudden we were overlooking the entire city. After we sat down and did our introductions—we were outnumbered by six to four—we began by asking some questions and were then able to review our proposal.

They asked about past performance and what technologies would we use. It turned out one of the things they liked about us was that we did not begin rattling off our capabilities. We turned it around on them, and I said, "There are a lot of things we need to know." One of the major areas we discovered was that security was paramount and every single product they used needed to be customized to work in their environment. Suddenly, we had to regroup and significantly change our tact. We boldly explained what they could not do, and they respected us for being forthright. I said, "We want to take a strategic view and see how we can tailor our proposal to your needs." We were taking a proactive role. We outlined how we would actually implement the project.

As I walked out of our four-hour meeting, the walls were not so intimidating anymore. On our plane ride back, I thought about what we accomplished and felt very positive about our meeting. It had been a long three days, and the day after we got back to St. Louis, we got a phone call awarding us the business! It was a $375,000 project. In a matter of four days, we won a very major account. We were under the gun and the rules of engagement were not favorable with a vaguely defined RFQ. Yet we worked the channels towards where we excelled.

What I learned: Display confidence that you are an expert and come across as such. Develop an ability to read the situation. Be persistent in marketing. Eventually, at some point in my life, they will need me and everything I say and do needs to set the stage for that. Understand the role you need to play and then act accordingly. Some people have an innate sales ability, being able to get along and relate to people on many levels. I still believe in the personal touch. Act with professionalism. Differentiate yourself. Small things can make a difference. The personal touch counts. Be a difference maker. Be real and sincere. Treat everyone with respect. Understand and take the time to listen to the client. Be in receiving mode and ask questions, walk in and know the industry. Find out how the client operates. Develop the relationship.

~

Angela Garland – President of Exit 11 Workspace, Coffee House & Drive-Thru

Angela built her company from scratch and she offered some excellent suggestions on what it takes to achieve success.

Being involved in the business community is invaluable. People want to do business with people they trust – which means they have to know who you are. Once they come to you, it is more the "experience" they have with your business than the product. They can get variations of your product anywhere, but they will come back to you if you make them feel important, welcome and create an experience that wows.

What I learned: There are some key characteristics and skills anyone in sales should have. Those include being authentic when developing relationships, understanding the different buying personalities so that you know how to communicate with them and following up; people aren't ignoring you, they are busy. So you have to stay in front of them. Own your mistakes and offer to make them right. We empower our employees to offer a free drink coupon for next time if we take too long or make a mistake with their order. The customer is always right, but not always for you. Know when to walk away from a selling/buying relationship that isn't working out.

~

John Gatewood – Co-Founder & President at Gatewood-Spalding Wealth Management

John is a successful financial planner and longtime insurance salesperson. He believes that a successful salesperson enjoys life, loves the challenge, and wakes up excited to meet the day.

There is some magic that happens when you talk to people. It boils down to your ability to communicate effectively. Great listeners are able to identify what is most important to the person. If you can gain a clear understanding of what it is the client wants to buy and interpret that, then you can guide them to what matches up perfectly to what they are thinking about.

God gave us two ears and one mouth to tell us that we need to listen twice as much as we speak. Good salespeople can tell you what they do in 30 seconds and why people should do business with them by describing the benefits to the client. They know how to keep a person engaged.

There is a fine line between being pleasantly persistent and rudely obnoxious. Until you cross over the line you don't know where it is. Simplicity is key to being a good salesperson. You have to have the ability to communicate complicated ideas in ways that are simple to grasp. Some people are auditory or visual or both, some need stories, some need analogies, some need numbers, comparison, statistics. Understanding what a person needs is an art form.

Great salespeople have an innate ability to catch that medium of communication that is most effective for each person. The greatest salespeople attribute their sales success to everyone else who helps them in the sale. For the great ones, failure is not an option. They do whatever it takes to be successful. You need to be willing and prepared to do whatever it takes to be successful. Learn from your mistakes, overcome defeats, do not become overwhelmed with the negatives, do not blame others or situations rather than simply accepting the fact, whatever happens, happens and then take personal responsibility.

What I learned: Drill down so you know the clients thoughts/feelings about the steps in their process for making a decision. When you break through relationship barriers or decision barriers, the relationship gets to a deeper level, a better level. If people are reluctant to talk about the most important things, how are you going to have a relationship with them? Some people are guarded and need more information before they begin giving it.

$\sim$

Andy Kanefield – Owner of Dialect, Inc., a strategic alignment firm

Andy was the principle in charge of branding at MKW, a mid-sized marketing firm. A prominent construction company was undergoing a brand make-over and they contacted Andy for his input. He learned that the potential client had already decided on hiring a strategic alignment company but before they put the final stamp on their proposal, they wanted MKW's thoughts on branding.

After further conversation, I learned the company called us because they had excellent feedback about our work from another reputable construction company, so it made sense to at least set up a meeting. As I drove to their headquarters, I kept thinking, is this an opportunity or are they just using us?

With that thought reverberating in my mind, I began by stating, "You have already selected another company, I'm sure they're very good, why not just go with them?" The managers appreciated my honesty and responded, "We have so much respect for our competitor and had heard your firm had done great work for them. Before we finalized our 'deal,' we want to know what MKW could do for us."

I then asked, "What benefit do we bring to the table that the other marketing company does not?" I wanted to see if they could quickly come up with another reason, why us. They commented, "We like your depth of experience and creativity."

After further discussion, it appeared they wanted to compare costs and see if they were getting a good deal. I forged on and said, "If the money was the same for each proposal, what would make the difference? You will know at the end of our meeting whether we are the right fit, whether we have the right chemistry, and at that point we can give you a full-blown proposal working side-by-side to create the best fit for your needs."

They were beginning to understand how we operated and I saw heads nodding in agreement. After further discussion and an understanding of our firm's capabilities, the client felt what I said about undertaking the proposal without knowing if we would get the business made a lot of sense.

The managers liked our company and committed to us that we should do the work. After fully into proposal mode, with the business supposedly in hand, I get a call from one of the general managers wanting to let me know that a relative (who is one of the partners in this family business) wanted more information prior to going any further.

I thought about this request for additional information. I decided not to supply the information and asked the managers, how actively did they want to be involved with branding—I was really pushing back and it was a gamble. They respected my response and felt this was the kind of firm they wanted for their branding make-over. We completed the proposal and finished the engagement. They subsequently became a long-term client.

What I learned: Reinforce the need to get to the client's issues; find out what is their pain. If you can't do that, don't go any farther. Pay attention to the red and yellow lights, and back out if it is not the right thing.

~

Bobbi Linkemer, Book writing coach and author

Bobbi is a writer and entrepreneur with a career spanning more than 30 years. She started her own writing business after writing for various companies and magazines. Her story is one of endurance, perseverance and just being herself. She has written 25 books and helped 27 authors write and publish their books. Her last 10 books have focused on how to write, publish and promote a nonfiction book.

I think it starts with me. I don't know that I would be any good with a product I didn't believe in. My first attempt at being a salesperson was in selling training for an international training and development company. I was great at soliciting needs. I was not a very good closer, actually I never closed a sale. I needed somebody to come up behind me and finish. When you are in your own business and you are selling you, you'd better be able to close the sale.

The product is me and the service is completely abstract. The client is not going to have something in their hands that they can touch and feel. The biggest challenge for me is having to audition over and over and over and prove myself not only to people who have not hired me before but to people I have worked with before. You're only as good as your last article, your last report, brochure, executive speech. "What have you done for me lately?" keeps ringing in my ears.

People ask me if I really understand their business and what makes me different. My challenge is using every opportunity presented to continue learning about their business. Foremost is being able to prove to new clients that I am a very quick study and I can delve inside their business and their minds. They don't want my style, they want *their* style. They want me to be them. And that is something I do well.

What I learned: You have to audition continuously. Every time I say hello to someone, it is essentially an audition. If they don't know you, they want to know what you've done and then they want to prove you can do it for them. My former clients believe in me and have invested some time in my learning curve but new clients want me to prove that I can really do what they want. Another challenge is having enough faith in myself. So I never say, "I can't do it." Someone asked me, "I need a marketing plan. Can you do that?" I replied, "Oh sure," despite the fact that I had never written a marketing plan in my life. I just went home and read a bunch of books on how to write a marketing plan and wrote down a proposal on how I would do it. Ask good questions, listen, give feedback. I build on everything I hear with another question or a summary of what I heard to be sure I understood what was said. When I meet with a client, and they think they want a brochure, that may not really be what they needed. Integrity is essential and one other trait is incredibly important: learning by watching what other people do. Be sincere and have a genuine interest in people.

$$\sim$$

Doug Pearson – Executive coach

Doug is an executive coach working with individuals and businesses to help them be more self-aware and ultimately, provide them an accountability source so they can achieve their dreams and goals. Doug's prospective client was named Ed, and he'd agreed to meet and work out the final arrangements for a coaching engagement. This would be a new client and Doug was looking forward to closing the deal.

I started the meeting by first asking Ed how did he want to begin and if there were any changes in his life since our last meeting. He became a bit defensive and said he didn't have the time and money to engage me in a coaching agreement at that time. And by the way, Ed was getting a divorce, with many issues both personal and professional. All of which prevented him from paying additional money for coaching.

I acknowledged Ed's remarks and did not get side-tracked by his claims but rather began asking him some further questions, really trying to clarify what his needs and major concerns were. After further questioning and listening, I decided to challenge Ed when I told him that the things that were holding him back in life were the very same things that held him back in engaging me as a coach. This seemed to resonate with him and he said he wanted to think this over and get back to me in a week.

I paused and looked Ed directly in the eyes and told him, "I will not permit you to think it over. Make a decision, yes or no." I knew Ed could make a decision if he was confronted with one to make then and there. He played the conversation over in his mind, hearing my advice and comments which I felt hit a cord and Ed seemed to know it as well. And they had. Ed signed an agreement to begin the coaching engagement starting the next week.

What I do is work with individuals to help them move forward and hopefully use the appropriate behavior with each client. In this case, it was directly confronting Ed and not letting him off the hook. It was the best thing for him and he knew it.

What I learned: Honesty—be honest with yourself. Integrity—keep your word, having the courage to confront. Sincerity—being real and authentic, taking a stand one way or the other. Vision—what are you here to contribute.

∾

Tim Rasmussen – Principal at Rivet|MRO

Tim was a program director for Maritz, a sales, marketing and employee motivation company. He was selling primarily to large, complex organizations. Maritz's corporate culture was such that it took pride in shaping proposals, a competitive edge. Tim uncovered an opportunity with Indiana's Hoosier Lottery. He and his team were confronted with something they weren't used to: Their competitor had previously established the ground rules for the upcoming RFP. Tim had to decide whether to compete or throw in the towel.

I prided myself in customer service and listening to the client's needs—what did they want to accomplish with their project, what were their "hot-buttons" and on and on. Had Maritz entered the competition too late? The competitor had the inside track. They had created the opportunity. We went to the customer and spent time asking many questions.

We employed what the Japanese call *kaizen* (continuous improvement) to find the root cause of a problem (asking the question "why" seven times).

This was a unique opportunity, which called for creativity. The proposal centered on giving away merchandise instead of cash—quite a different approach for a lottery. I felt like we were entering the game too late. The competition had the upper hand. Yet after intense listening and further examination of the RFP, we determined what the customer wanted was extraordinarily complicated and we felt we had a unique capability to deliver. We could craft a proposal to play off our strengths and the competitor's weaknesses.

We invested a great deal of time and effort preparing the response by brainstorming, generating creative ideas and really adding value. Our end product was more than 300 pages. It still bothered me that our competitors were in first, but after reviewing our proposal, I felt confident we had a solid deliverable. And so did the client. We were awarded the business, worth $5 million.

Our team had out-thought and out-worked the competition. We answered all the specifications and minor details, and really provided added value. We gave them more than what they asked for and really reshaped the landscape. Our team created an ironclad system to meet their needs. Maritz recognized our efforts and built off the success of this situation, creating a whole new line of business focusing on lotteries as a vertical market resulting in millions of dollars more of additional business.

What I learned: Think things through and find the issues that underlie what they are asking for. Go to the next level and really give the customer what they need. Continue to ask the question "Why?" Find out what they want, what they need and why they need it. What are you trying to accomplish? It's not being product-focused, its being customer-focused; being solution-oriented, finding out what the customer thinks the problem is, then peeling back each layer of the onion and finding out the real problem. What is underneath it?—because quite often it isn't as apparent as it seems. Service mentality is critical; solving problems for people. People don't buy stuff, they buy solutions. It requires not only listening and asking questions; it requires somebody to bend over backwards and really dig in and then a couple of things result. You wind up with a better solution, and you show a lot more about your willingness to help, building greater credibility and trust.

$$\sim$$

Jimmy Steiner – Senior Wealth Advisor, Mosaic Family Wealth and former sports agent
Jim was a great sports agent for more than 35 years in a very tough business. He's seen it all, like the time he went to a client's apartment and the player's pet snake was slithering around loose.

Deuce McAllister (former New Orleans Saints running back) was a pretty monumental get for us. Deuce went to Ole Miss so he had retained an attorney in Jackson to screen all the candidates to serve as his agent. All the top agency people in the business had to make presentations to the attorney. I first went down and met with the attorney, then we had to make a presentation at his office to his staff, Deuce and several family members.

We were going into the deep south trying to sign an African-American running back which was a real challenge for us because we had never been to Ole Miss before. His mother was involved—his mother and father were divorced—so we had to deal with the attorneys, we were dealing with Deuce, we were dealing with family members and there were a lot of people involved. We ended up making a memorable presentation and signing him.

The Jerry Rice (former San Francisco 49ers wide receiver and Pro Football Hall of Fame inductee) story was a good one. He came in the league in 1985 and in 1986, Roger Craig (former running back) called and said, "I have a new client for you." I asked who and he said Jerry Rice. I replied, "I'll be there in about 10 minutes." Jerry was just getting started. He was in his second year with the 49ers at the time so he was not the greatest yet. I signed him on the first visit. He was having some trouble with his previous agent. That was one of those things that happen very quickly and then after 19 years and millions of dollars later in fees we were still working with him. We maintained Jerry because of excellent service. It's one thing to get a client, it's another to keep them.

Sometimes your best accounts are the easiest sales. Common sense and good service are keys. Then the older they get, the less service they need. You have to really hug them early in the relationship. It's sort of like a marriage, its puppy love and then after a while, it's, "Hi honey, I'm home!"

How we got Daryl Strawberry (former New York Mets outfielder) is a good story because he was a high school player at the time, a very well-known player and we read about him in *Sports Illustrated*. This was in the very early years when we had nobody, and we called Los Angeles directory assistance to get a number for his mother, Ruby Strawberry. We got the number and I cold-called and said I was going to L.A. and I wanted to meet with her. I remembered meeting her at a Hamburger Hamlet on Wilshere Blvd.

So I met with her first, and at that point I only had a couple of years in the business. We took Ruby and Darryl to the Dodger game and took them up to the broadcast booth to see the legendary broadcaster Jack Buck and we signed Darryl. Out of all the agents who were swarming around L.A., on a whim, we got his mother's phone number, went to visit her and we signed him.

What I learned: Be tenacious and aggressive. Have good follow up and communication skills, be able to adapt to all different types of situations, understand who the decision makers are. Be incredibly resilient, have no fear, have a good sense of timing, know when to get out, know when to shut it down. It's all about developing relationships. Establish a relationship with whoever your target is. If you are successful at that you have a reasonable chance of making the sale. Once the relationship is established it comes with trust, credibility and that is the foundation of a successful partnership.

"The fact is, everyone is in sales."

— Jay Abraham

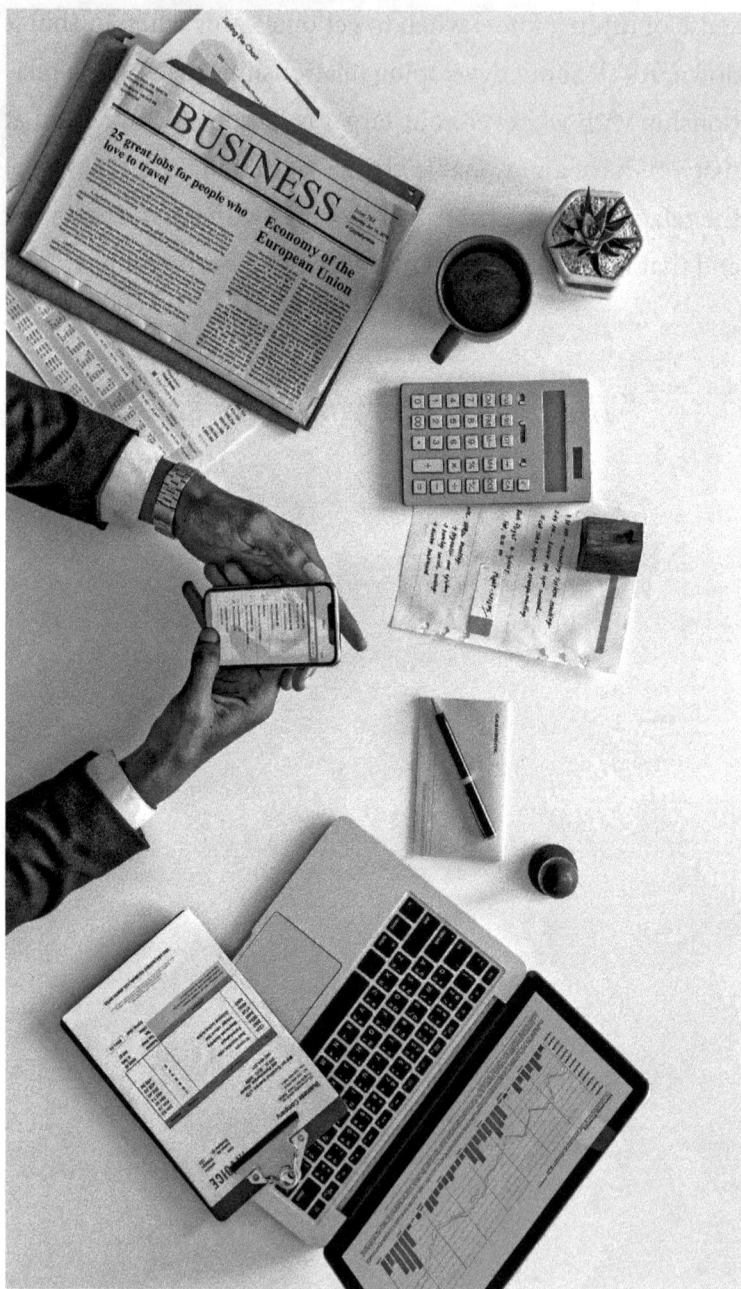

Chapter 12

Epilogue:
How The Sales Process Has Changed And Where It's Going

When I first came up with the idea to write a book about sales, I was embedded in technology—selling processors for mainframe applications. I had success in my career because I was selling a superior product and I had a top notch service and support team standing behind that product.

I saw a lot of changes in the sales process during my career. During the past couple of decades, those changes have affected the way all of us buy and sell products. It's also impacted the way we conduct research about products. There was a time when if you were in the market for a car, you went into a dealer, took a test drive, did a bit of haggling and settled on a price.

That's still an option. Some buyers prefer to buy cars that way. However, changes have already emerged in recent years. Sites like Autotrader.com and Cars.com are disrupting the traditional car buying experience. More and more, internet sales are controlling the way people buy autos. In 2018, 22% of car buyers used a social media site as a source while shopping for a new vehicle. That reflects an increase of 6% in just three years.[1]

One thing hasn't changed, though. Most car buyers are undecided at the beginning of the shopping process. That's an interesting fact because as a salesperson, one of our primary goals is to remove *fear, uncertainty and doubt* from our buyer's mind. Whether it be a car, laundry detergent or a computer, many buyers are undecided or uncertain about buying. A good salesperson can paint a word picture for the customer and describe how by buying your product or service, you will have made a wise purchase.

In a web-based sales world, the model many of us grew up with no longer exists. That's particularly true for consumer retail sales. Shopping malls are ghost towns. Macy's and J. C. Penney have closed hundreds of stores. The once mighty giant retailer Sears barely exists.

What has emerged in place of those diminished brands is a democratized marketplace, where anybody who has a good idea for a product or service can achieve some level of success. Now, platforms like eBay, Etsy and Amazon allow buyers and sellers to connect and complete transactions online. There is no face-to-face selling involved. Sellers still have to provide buyers with the confidence that the product is of good quality. How do they do that? Often, through positive reviews, the holy grail of online sellers. Again, it removes uncertainty in the mind of the buyer.

---

[1] Source: Autotrader.com research - https://www.v12data.com/blog/25-amazing-statistics-on-how-consumers-shop-for-cars/

Online selling has become the great equalizer, allowing anyone to market their product. In fact, this has opened up an entirely new way for creative people armed with little more than an idea to achieve success. "Build a better mousetrap and the world will beat a path to your door" is how Ralph Waldo Emerson put it the late nineteenth century. That saying holds true today even if the way you sell the mousetrap has changed drastically.

What impact does the transition to an impersonal, online sales experience have for face-to-face sales? Does it marginalize or diminish the importance of building a relationship with a customer and learning about them, forming a connection?

I will be so bold as to say our growing reliance on e-commerce is actually a positive for salespeople like myself and others profiled in this book. We have at our command a limitless amount of information about our customers and their markets, which we can access with a few keystrokes. Our ability to learn more about who we're selling to can make us better salespeople. We now have the tools to really understand the customer's business and what their needs are.

Pam Fisher, who was profiled in the "Five Ps" chapter 8, wisely suggested that reliance on specialization is a huge change over the last couple of years. Customers, she said, "Don't want to buy a quarter inch drill, they want a quarter inch hole, so we need to figure out how to bridge that need and how to sell to them a product or service that will accomplish it."

Jeff Loeb, who we met in the "Professional Persistence" chapter 3 and "Think Outside The Box" chapter 6, suggests that the nature of sales has changed drastically in the dot com era.

"More and more, sales today are direct to the end user via the internet (e-commerce), rather than through a third party (interacting with a buyer at a brick and mortar retail store). A sale direct to consumer through Amazon.com, for example, does not carry a barrier of setting up an appointment or coordinating the sale through a third party buyer. However, such a direct e-commerce sale does assume a larger marketing responsibility of engaging the consumer (which is forfeited if one's product is seen on a retail shelf if transacted through a brick and mortar store).

"With my startup company, I'm selling via both e-commerce and brick and mortar. I am spending 90% of my time on social media to engage consumers on-line with the hope of converting those interactions into on-line sales. Social media marketing requires similar message techniques that always work well: You've got to be concise. You've got two seconds to get the customer's attention. They're not going to read three paragraphs, so you've got to grab their attention quickly, and that's sales."

Pam Fisher also told me something that should resonate with all salespeople. It's never a good idea to take shortcuts or lose sight of your values. There's a tendency among some salespeople who are under intense pressure to meet their sales quotas to play fast and loose with numbers. It may sound a little corny, she said, but "I had a saying that worked well for me: 'Take the high road.' I had salespeople who told me later years, 'I hated you when you said take the high road,' but the reality is that advice has never served me badly. So do what's right."

Kevin Hollenbach, who we met in chapter 9, echoed Jeff Loeb's opinion that one of the biggest impacts on sales and selling in the past decade has been social media. Kevin told me, "It boggles my mind that reps don't arm themselves with the wealth of information that's available when they walk in to call on a customer. With LinkedIn premium services, you can find out what the buyer's interests are, and all kinds of details about the company. There is so much information that's available before you ever show up. Some people are extremely successful using it. That's a big weapon that should be used more.

"It's also important to remember that the fundamentals still apply. You've got to develop solid relationships. And having a good work ethic is extremely important. I always try to figure out a candidate's work ethic when I interview people and it's not always easy. When they have that drive and desire, it can make all the difference in the world because at the end of the day, the one who makes the most calls, wins."

Another excellent piece of advice for salespeople is to accept defeat gracefully and learn from that experience. This wisdom came from Patti Harty, who's noteworthy sales experience was featured in "What do you have to lose?" in chapter 2. Patti said that there will be instances where you lose business, but whining and complaining about it serves little purpose. "You've just got to get back to the basics, blocking and tackling," she said. "You can't just complain that you didn't make your quota. You've got to get back off of the mat and get back in the game and play."

Sales, as you can probably tell, is a subject we salespeople love to analyze and philosophize about. I hope this book has provided you with some insight into the sales process, offered some useful advice about achieving your own sales goals, and maybe even made you smile.

"We make a living by what we get but we make a life by what we give."

– Winston Churchill

Appendix

Tools You Can Use

I credit my success in sales to a number of factors. Not the least of those was working alongside many dedicated team members who had my back, like my friend and colleague Kevin Hollenbach, who offered expert technical guidance and support during our careers. I could always count on Kevin then, and even now, as he provided some great stories in Chapter 9. My mentor and former boss Jim Grimmit (who penned the Foreword of this book) also provided critical support to me in my sales days, as did Bill Davis, noted in chapter 4.

When you establish a network and support system early in your career, you will continue to reap rewards and benefits. A great salesperson should acquire, nurture and cherish those contacts. A great salesperson should also continue to improve his or her skills, through development opportunities like those offered by Sandler Training.

There is one other thing that I cannot stress strongly enough for a great salesperson. That is preparation. Throughout this book, Jeff Loeb, Pam Fisher and others emphasized this important detail. Your likelihood of closing a sale will be much greater if you adequately prepare for a sales presentation or even just a first meeting with a potential customer. You could back up even further and prepare yourself for the first phone call you make to a customer, who may not know you at all. Your objective is to learn everything you can about that person and his or her company. It is an ongoing process and the more you meet with the customer, the more you will learn.

When you do uncover new information about your customer, write it down immediately and keep it in a file that is easy to access. It's your call as to what format is best. Some salespeople keep data in an Excel spreadsheet and others carefully write in longhand using a leather bound journal. I always took copious notes and still do; now I use the notepad app on my iPhone to enter this type of information. Everybody has their own preference. You could write short entries on post-it notes and stick them all over your office. That might not be the most efficient method; hey, everybody is different and organizes their thoughts and information in ways that best suit them.

The important thing is to obtain the information and look over it when you are preparing to meet with a customer. When you demonstrate to your customer that you know or remember something relevant about that person and his or her company, it shows a level of commitment on your part. It shows that you view the person that you cared enough to remember an upcoming birthday or other milestone. This type of personal attention is significant because it will make you stand out from other salespeople who don't go that extra step. Amazingly, many do not. You don't want to be that person.

What information should you collect? It can range from personal information about your contact to information about their company that you can obtain from many online sources. You can create and modify a list of information and data that works best for you. Or, feel free to use my own creation—what I call the C3 for the "Cornbleet Customer Checklist," which I've provided below.

In each of the three C sections you'll find 12 key fields to complete. Some are relatively easy to get the information about. It will take a few minutes and a quick Google search. For others, you'll need to talk to people, ask questions and listen carefully. Why 36 points? The number has a bit of symmetry and let's face it, we salespeople can be as superstitious as anyone. Keep in mind that the number 36 has a bit of mystical significance. According to the ancient Midrash, the light created by God on the first day of creation shone for exactly 36 hours.

I encourage you to create your own version of the C3. It might have a variety of other factors I didn't include. The main rule is to listen, learn and remember. Then, use all of this valuable information as you prepare for a sales meeting. As the restaurant impresario Danny Meyer wrote in his excellent book "Setting The Table," you should follow the ABCD rule—that is, "Always Be Connecting Dots."

And here's one more piece of valuable advice—consider this lagniappe (the New Orleans term for "a little gift"): Be early. Not just on time. Green Bay Packers legendary coach Vince Lombardi considered a player or coach "late" if they arrived at practice less than 15 minutes before the scheduled start time. There are some good reasons for you to do likewise. The extra time will allow you to gather your thoughts, calm yourself and portray confidence. Your customer will appreciate it, too, since many of your competitors won't provide this important courtesy.

C3 Cornbleet Customer Checklist

C1 - Company Information

1. Company Name _____

2. Website _____

3. Public or Private _____

4. Business Sector _____

5. Customer Base _____

6. Mission and Strategy
   [often available on company website]

   _____

7. HQ Location _____

8. Previous Year Revenue _____
   [you can find this information from hoovers.com]

9. FORTUNE 500 Ranking [fortune.com/global500]

   _____

10. DiversityInc Top 50 Ranking _____
    [diversityinc.com/di_top_50]

11. Customer's Primary Competition _____
    [available from hoovers.com]

    _____

12. Competitive Differentiator _____

C2 - People Information

1. Key Decision Maker Name _____

2. Level of Autonomy _____

3. Phone/Cell Numbers _____

4. Email address _____

5. Age/Birthday _____

6. College Attended _____

7. Favorite Sports Team _____

8. Family Member's Names and Ages _____

_____

9. Hobbies _____

10. Background
    [you can find this information from Linkedin.com]

_____

11. Career Goals [Linkedin.com] _____

12. Linkedin Profile _____

C3 – Intangible Information

1. Corporate Culture _____

2. Key Opportunities _____

3. Potential Conflicts _____

4. Potential Objections _____

5. Counter Arguments To Address Objections

   _____

6. Customer In Growth, Expansion or Survival Mode

   _____

7. Allies/Sponsors With Unique Knowledge of Customer

   _____

8. Decision Maker's Admin or Gatekeeper Name

   _____

9. Everything In C2 Section About Decision Maker's Admin or Gatekeeper Name

   _____

10. Preferred mode of communication
    (email, text, voice mail) _____

11. Your Company's Competition For Customer's Business

    _____

12. Your Company's Competitive Differentiator

    _____

Acknowledgments

There are many people who have helped in small and large ways in making this book happen.

My collaborator, Bill Motchan who made the words flow and brought the stories to life. Thank you.

Cathy and Jack Davis who brought the book to press and introduced me to Bill—you have been incredibly helpful.

To Mary Kutheis who introduced me to Cathy and encouraged me to proceed with my outline and vignettes— you are an inspiration and well respected for writing a book yourself.

To my sales colleagues and friends for their support— words are not adequate to thank you. The people cited in this book: Patti Harty, my friend since birth and superb salesperson—you are the best. Jeff Loeb—another long-time friend who loves a good story, especially having to do with fish—I appreciate all you do (plus being the brains behind our fantasy football team). Pam Fisher, what a great contributor from your AT&T experience—thanks for your willingness to participate. Chris Herrington, a serendipitous "find"— thanks for a wonderful story and insights. My right hand guy, Kevin Hollenbach in many memorable sales—your technical support was invaluable "in my day" and the incredible success you have had and continue to have is truly exceptional: Great job!

Many thanks to the 13 salespeople I interviewed for the "What They Learned" chapter: Suzie Andrews, Hal Becker, Bev Berner, Adam Capes, Tom Cohn, Patrick Garrett, Angela Garland, John Gatewood, Andy Kanefield, Bobbi Linkemer, Doug Pearson, Tim Rasmussen and Jimmy Steiner, your stories were fascinating and inspirational.

I had many excellent mentors/coaches in my years selling so thanks to all of them. Two that stand out: Jim Grimmet and Bill Davis—what incredible men, both in the sales "game" and life. You taught and challenged me—these stories and life would not be the same without you. Also many thanks to Grimmet for writing the foreword.

Suzy, my loving wife of 40+ years who has stuck with me through "thick and thin." I cannot tell you how much you mean to me (even saying: "Why don't you treat family like you treat your customers..."). Amy and Molly, our daughters, who have grown into incredible women and I could not be prouder to be your dad. Janey, thanks for being a patient and kind sister. Josh, my wonderful son-in-law, thanks for taking good care of my daughter Amy. Kai and Sterling, I get to learn and play and watch you grow—nothing better than twin g-boys!

About the Author

Jim Cornbleet is a first-time author. His book "Who Says A Fish Can't Sell?" is a reflection on his life as a salesman, and experiences of other top salespeople. He tells an entertaining tale of what it takes to be a great salesperson, offering an inside look at the process, and most important, key learnings.

A career in sales was not something Jim Cornbleet ever imagined. His father was a furniture salesman who counseled Jim to find a job doing something more concrete and stable. Jim earned his undergrad degree in accounting. What could be more stable than that?

He was hired by Monsanto as a cost accountant, and while on the job he continued his studies, earning an MBA degree from Washington University. There was only one problem. He found he had no passion for accounting—he jokes that he only knew debits were on the left and credits were on the right.

Jim made a bold move and left Monsanto and went to work for IBM because he thought technology was the future. It was 1982 and he couldn't have been more correct in his assessment. In 1987 Jim was hired by Amdahl to knock on doors and sell the product of the future.

He quickly figured out it was the right move. He was a born salesman. Jim loved the job because it gave him a chance to meet and work with a variety of people and to hone his listening skills. Listening, he learned, was one of the most important skills a salesperson can cultivate. He also found he could earn a good living.

Jim has also worked in strategic planning, sales and executive coaching with small and mid-sized companies in the construction, professional services, and technology industries. Jim started his own company—Network for You, Inc.—a revolutionary new concept in professional services that gives business owners access to top-notch providers in sales management and development, marketing, strategic planning and executive coaching.

When he's not teaching, coaching or writing, you can find Jim at the golf course, or working tirelessly on community service and social service projects. He has shared his compassion for others as the development director for Sherwood Forest for five years and serving on the boards of Progressive Youth Center, Archway Communities, Cystic Fibrosis, the Science Center Development Committee, Camp for All Kids, AFP and Big Brothers Big Sisters of Greater St. Louis.

Jim's wife Suzy is an Associate Professor in Physical Therapy at Washington University in St. Louis.. The Cornbleets have two daughters: Amy who owns Mammography Educators in San Diego; and Molly, public affairs director for Abbott in San Francisco.